To Biddy
May you [illegible]
you read
Rae Neal
September 11, 2016

Midnight Melodies

From the Seas and Rivers of Life

RAE NEAL

xulon PRESS

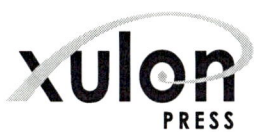

Copyright © 2014 by Rae Neal

Midnight Melodies
From the Seas and Rivers of Life
by Rae Neal

Printed in the United States of America

ISBN 9781498416047

All rights reserved solely by the author. The author guarantees all contents are original and do not infringe upon the legal rights of any other person or work. No part of this book may be reproduced in any form without the permission of the author. The views expressed in this book are not necessarily those of the publisher.

Unless otherwise indicated, Scripture quotations are taken from the King James Version (KJV) – public domain

Scripture quotations are taken from the New King James Version (NKJV). Copyright © 1979, 1980, 1982 by Thomas Nelson, Inc. Used by permission. All rights reserved.

Scripture quotations are taken from the New American Standard Bible (NASB). Copyright © 1960, 1962, 1963, 1968, 1971, 1972, 1973, 1975, 1977, 1995 by The Lockman Foundation. Used by permission. All rights reserved.

www.xulonpress.com

Dedication

This book must be dedicated to those I love most in my life. Since God is my life's center focus without whom there would be no book, I willingly begin my dedication to Him. He has granted me life from the womb and in my adult years, He has given me purpose, but most of all, He has given me His Spirit of inspirations and His amazing love. He makes me laugh! I owe Him everything.

To my son, David, I dedicate the legacy of this book. He has always been the light of my life and a source of countless joys since he was born and still is. When the Lord speaks through him, I listen.

To my son, Lance, I wish I could dedicate this book's legacy to him, as well. But, he makes his home with our Lord in heaven, for which I am grateful since it means we will be together again some joy-filled day.

The delights of my life are my three granddaughters. I dedicate my writings to them and pray they will use them to always keep me as near to their hearts as they are to mine: gorgeous Lauren; so very pretty Tara; beautiful Molly. You fill my thoughts and have my love always.

I dedicate this delightful distraction to my husband and friend, Terry, who has been so patient and listened to every word written and has always been an encouragement with his descriptive words, "Deep!" or "Uh huh, I get it!"

To my twin sister, Kay, I dedicate the toil of this poetic endeavor for believing in me from the deepest beginnings considering we were one egg which split and we became two. Our lives have always proven:

two halves can be better than one whole! Only God can explain how intertwined identical twins' lives are from conception.

My dedication of Midnight Melodies: *From the Seas and Rivers of Life* also goes to the rest of my family and all of my friends; those with whom I grew up in Cushing and are still "draggin' Main." Thank you for your love and patience in contending with all of my doubts as well as my certainties.

My prayer is that God bless you with the knowledge of His love and mine.

Acknowledgments

My deepest gratitude goes to a childhood friend, Rev. Bracy Ball, who loves the Lord enough to say "Yes" to the challenge of jumping into the role as Editor. His organized and detailed reports kept me moving forward when my late night or all night commitments to meet the deadline were cause for bleary-eyed mistakes. Bracy's gifted eye with attention to the minutia and his sacrifice of time the work required has been a huge blessing. My thanks to his wife, Raylene, too, for allowing this project to intervene in their lives. Thank you to both of them for much needed prayers.

I gratefully acknowledge those whose support and encouragement have kept the "author's fire" lit not only through friendship, but through their prayers: Jerry Long, Cheryl Weisler, Tommy Rogers, Mandy Moody and especially my niece, Stacy Hardin, and her Mother, my twin sister, Kay Zumwalt.

An acknowledgment goes to Dr. Rich Ventonis for mentoring me in the early years of God's calling on my life. Thank you, Rich, for all the invaluable advice, spiritual guidance and faith in God's giftings in my life. Many of your instructive words still pop into my mind from time to time.

Thanksgiving has an enduring existence in my heart through my ancestors for the legacy of Christian believers in Christ and service to the Lord in ministry whose long line of names is too numerous to mention. There is something to be said about the passage of blessings and the callings of God through the generations.

Table of Contents

Dedication .... *v*
Acknowledgments .... *vii*
Foreword .... *xiii*
Foreword .... *xv*
About the Author .... *xvii*
Introduction .... *xxi*

Midnight Melodies 27
A Cup of Water 29
A Life, Dance 31
A Moment and a Day Forever 33
Another Day to Feed the World 35
A Trip To The Beach 37
Baked in Your Love 39
Blessed Whispers 41
Call to Battle 43
Cantaloupe 45
Colors of Life 47
Come Up High 49
Crazy Love 51
Dark Shadows 53
Discovery of God's Designs 55
Dreaming 57

Dreams Don't Die	59
Flashes of Parenthood	63
Fools Go Down	67
Footsteps in Front of Me	69
Friends Together	71
Gentlemen, Come Blow Your Trumpets	73
God's Breath	77
Gotta Walk the Cair Someday	79
Gratitude	81
Heaven's Music	83
He is Life	85
Her Great Love	87
His Bride	89
His Voice Calls	91
Imaginations	93
In The Twilight	95
Leaves	97
Left Behind	99
Light Side, Dark Side	101
Love's First Bloom	105
Mirror, Mirror	107
Mystery	109
No More Good-Byes	111
No More Time	115
Ocean of Life	117
Ouch!	119
Please	121
Practice	123

Question...125
Release of a Saint 127
Remember 129
Speak..131
Such a Name!..133
Swept Into Her Future 135
Take A Little Walk With Me.............................137
Teardrops and Diamonds.................................139
The Creator's One-At-A-Time 141
The Exchange...143
The False Accusation 145
The Free Ride...149
The Joy of Pain 151
The Midnight Hour.....................................153
The Smile of a Child 155
The Throes of Grief 157
The Unknown 159
The Word 161
Truth Wins!...163
Voices of Martyrs 165
Weeping in the Heavens.................................167
"What Meaneth This?"..................................169
Whispers of Love 171
Who Are You Robin Hood?..............................173
Who Cares?..175
My King 177

Foreword

The pleasant surprises of life are often unexpected. This poetry collection meets that description, as you will discover as you journey through its pages.

This book will resurrect memories from your younger days as well as heighten your expectations for the future. Many aspects of your life will intersect with the personalized perspectives of the many insightful and heartwarming poems. Some poems will prompt you to contemplate the wisdom, purposes, and understanding of a personal God in this world and in your life. The blessings, the questions, the surprises, and the wonder of your existence are intertwined in the moving word pictures of these poems.

The ability that the author, Rae (Carter) Neal, brings to this presentation is refreshing and insightful. Her life experiences began in Cushing, a small oil town in Oklahoma, and continued through college, to Europe, to the capital of Russia, to the volcanic mountain villages of Guatemala and even to responsibilities on an Atlantic Ocean island off the coast of West Africa. All of these locations, among others, along with inevitable joys and disappointments of everyday life, provided a rich and varied background from which an awesome and in-depth perspective of life has been fashioned. When you read Rae's poems, you will read her words . . . But you will also be peering into her heart.

I am an admirer of Rae as a person. We attended school together, from elementary through high school. We lost touch with one another for many years but then reconnected even though we live half a continent apart. In her book, I believe you will reconnect with your own path of memories and realize a greater appreciation for life that has hope for the present as well as the future.

It is a privilege for me to write about the impact and beauty of Rae Neal's poetry and to recommend **Midnight Melodies: *From the Seas and Rivers of Life*.** She is truly blessed with amazing creativity and unique communication skills, as you will discover.

—Bracy Ball, Las Vegas, Nevada, President of Word Truth Ministries http://WWW.wordtruth.net

Foreword

Recently my childhood family friend, Rae (Carter) Neal, asked me to read her upcoming book, **Midnight Melodies: *From the Seas and Rivers of Life.*** As I read through her manuscript, I was reminded of the Scriptures in Ecclesiastes 3.

[1] To everything *there is* a season,
A time for every purpose under heaven:
[2] A time to be born, And a time to die;
A time to plant, And a time to pluck *what is* planted;
[3] A time to kill, And a time to heal;
A time to break down, And a time to build up;
[4] A time to weep, And a time to laugh;
A time to mourn, And a time to dance;
[5] A time to cast away stones, And a time to gather stones;
A time to embrace, And a time to refrain from embracing;
[6] A time to gain, And a time to lose;
A time to keep, And a time to throw away;
[7] A time to tear, And a time to sew;
A time to keep silence, And a time to speak;
[8] A time to love, And a time to hate;
A time of war, And a time of peace.

In life we are presented with many joys and sorrows, healings and pains, life and death. In life's experiences, some we choose and some we do not, we do experience them. Reading through Rae's book, **Midnight Melodies: *From the Seas and Rivers of Life*** we have the opportunity to share in many of life's experiences, a few of her own, as the good and the not so good times of life are eloquently expressed. As I read her poetic reflections of life, I was reminded of many of my own life experiences and how God had been in the midst of each one whether I had recognized it or not.

Rae Neal's book, insightfully written and easily relatable, will give you a thought provoking time of reflection for your own life or others you know. God's goodness and His plan for our lives are *"for good and not for evil, to give us a future and a hope."* It is in the quiet times we take to spend time with Him that we find our Source of hope for the hopeless, strength for the weak, joy for the mourning, and steps for the future. In a world where we daily hear of the evil, we are reminded that there is hope in the Creator of our life. I encourage you to read **Midnight Melodies: *From the Seas and Rivers of Life*** with an open heart and a listening ear to hear the still quiet voice of our Father sharing His love for His child, you!

Dr. John Benefiel; Founder and Senior Pastor, Church on the Rock, Oklahoma City; Vice-President, Church on the Rock International; Presiding Apostle, Heartland Apostolic Prayer Network and Oklahoma Apostolic Prayer Network; Author, *Binding The Strongman Over America*

About the Author

Rae Neal saw God's future for her life when she was 10 years old. She was strolling homeward at dusk on a warm summer evening with her twin sister, Kay. They were known as the Carter twins. In the crook of Rae's left arm were cradled her piano books of classical music and her right hand gripped Kay's left hand. They had been to their weekly piano lesson in the home of their teacher, Mrs. Moses.

Suddenly, Rae became aware of how the road stretched seemingly forever in front of them beyond a hazy horizon. She felt embraced by a warm-like presence cocooning her with a gooey love that spread over her like molasses. She began to speak quietly, but with strong conviction, *"Katie, see the end of this road in the distance? There are far away lands beyond it, countries where other people live. I feel like God is going to take me to live way out there in the world somewhere. He has a work for me to do someday in those distant lands."* Quickly, Kay jerked on her hand and exclaimed with trepidation in her voice, *"Stop talking like that, Raetie, you're scaring me!"*

With a sense of sisterly protection, Rae did just that, but her thoughts were filled with the compelling needs of strangers beyond their small world and they hung in the air around her until they arrived home. Their parents and younger brother, Charles, were awaiting them at the dinner table laden with pot roast and vegetables from the backyard garden. The aura of a definitive destiny laid out for her by God was soon forgotten until many years later. Through many twists and turns, that future finally materialized.

Years later, Rae was praising the Lord as she sang in the spirit in the shower. She was startled to hear a soft but firm voice begin to speak to her spirit these words, *"Prepare, Rae, for I'm going to send you to far away lands and there you will preach, teach and heal my people."* So began her preparations for full-time ministry as a foreign missionary. She went through Bible College while she volunteered in her church. When she became an ordained minister with the Assemblies of God, she received her first assignment to the foreign mission field.

Rae was appointed to Pastor two churches simultaneously in the Canary Islands of Spain. The locations of the churches were only fifteen minutes apart, so it was really no different than preaching multiple services in a church in the United States.

The church in San Agustin was in a Chapel which was built next to the beach in front of the Atlantic Ocean and the church in Playa del Ingles was a half block from the beach. Many tourists would hear Rae preaching through outdoor speaker systems attached to the buildings and walk into the services out of curiosity. Both men and women would be dressed in their bikini bathing suits.

Her first Sunday morning in the pulpits of those two churches was the beginning of learning many ministry lessons from the Lord. The Spirit of God let her know that she was to never be concerned about the number of people in a service or Bible study, how much the financial offerings were or how much or how little clothing the people were wearing. From then on, those three orders were never a problem for her. She spoke God's Word to a small congregation near a dusty garbage dump in Mexico and to over 25,000 people while standing on the platform of an arena in St. Petersburg, Russia.

A dear lady in a Assembly of God church in Stillwater, Oklahoma, told Rae early in her ministry career that the Lord had *"set before you an open door that no man can shut."* Revelation 3:8. Through the years, God opened doors for her to preach and teach in foreign countries in churches, prisons, orphanages, schools, tin buildings, town centers, tents, hospitals, nursing homes and theaters. Those locations were in such varied places as a remote, jungle clearing in the mountains of Guatemala to a gypsy church in Slovakia to a Church of England cathedral near London. Everywhere she was sent by the call of God, she was in situations where precious people were in need of the message of the Word of God. She witnessed the power of God save spiritually needy people, heal their diseases and physical problems and deliver them from addictions and demonic possessions.

In 2003, Rae married Terry Neal and they make their home in Tulsa, Oklahoma. Several years ago, her life began to change once again. Her inspirations to write poetically began when she was awakened in the night by the Spirit of God with words gushing up from her spirit with such force she could not go back to sleep until she wrote them down. She never really gave the writings very much thought until family and friends began encouraging her to publish them. They finally prevailed upon her to submit several entries in a Christian Writer's Contest of Xulon Press in February, 2014. God is full of surprises. Three of her free-verse poems were given Honorable Mention. Being encouraged with that honor, she decided to enter again in June. This time she was awarded a Third Place prize. So began the vision for this book, Midnight Memories: *From the Seas and Rivers of Life*. It is her desire that you be blessed and transported through the seas and rivers of your life, in part, through this book's inspirations.

A bit of past history:
- Minister of Adult Singles, Woodlake Assembly of God, Tulsa, OK
- Pastor of two churches on Grand Canary Island, Spain: San Agustin Chapel, San Augustin, and Templo Ecumenico, Playa del Ingles
- Pastor of Mijas Evangelical Church in Mijas, southern Spain
- Ministered in several locations in Mexico; preached and taught in various locations in Guatemala for Living Waters

Ministries; preached a 10-day crusade in Costa Rica; launched and taught in Victory Bible Institute, St. Petersburg, Russia, immediately after the USSR was dissolved; laid the groundwork by teaching seminars and preaching throughout Czech Republic and Slovakia for the opening of a Rhema Bible College; guest speaker in southern England churches
- Associate in Pastoral Ministry for several years, Sheepshed Fellowship, Sand Springs, OK
- Currently the Pastor for the past five years, Church at Mansion House complex, Tulsa, OK.
- Rae was ordained with the Assemblies of God. After resigning and joining an independent, missionary sending agency, she has been ordained and licensed by several organizations.

Education:
- Business: Blackwood Business College, Oklahoma City, Oklahoma (now closed)
- Rhetoric and Writing Major: Tulsa University, Tulsa, Oklahoma
- Ministerial Studies Major: Berean Bible College (now Global University), Springfield, Missouri
- Missions: Victory World Missions Training Center, Tulsa, Oklahoma (now Victory School of Missions)

Member:
- Heartland Apostolic Prayer Network
- Oklahoma Apostolic Prayer Network
- 24/31 Tulsa Area Prayer Network

Introduction

The title of my book of poetical expressions was inspired by what I call, *"one of those blessing moments."* I had been living on Grand Canary Island of Spain for over two years. During that time, I had not heard thunder, seen rain or lightning. One night a clap of thunder awakened me from a deep sleep shortly after midnight. It took a clap or two before I comprehended what was occurring. Then I leapt from my bed and ran out onto the front terrace of my tiny apartment which overlooked the Atlantic Ocean. I sat snuggled in a terrace chair most of the night until around 4:00am when the storm out over the ocean could not be seen any longer.

When a missionary leaves their family, friends and their own country to live in a land where they have never visited, among a people and culture they do not know or have any acquaintance with, the missionary expects to experience what is known as *"Culture Shock."* We learn in our training that there are many adjustments which must be made. Two years is considered the usual amount of exposure to an unfamiliar culture to finally become settled in and nesting, putting down a few roots by gaining friendships and decorating your living quarters with your own personal touches. Some missionaries adjust more quickly than others. A close relationship with the Lord does not always determine how swiftly a person will adjust, but it does help you to endure the transition.

From time to time, a missionary will discover something they are missing from home. Perhaps that something will not even be noticed for quite awhile, then suddenly an incident will prompt a realization of what is missing. That is what happened to me the night of *"the storm."*

Summertime has always been my favorite season of the year. The temperature can never climb too high for me. I love the sun, the warm to hot days and almost any body of water. God knows everything there is to know about each of us individually. When the phone call came and I was informed that I would be going to live on this unusual, volcanic island surrounded by the Atlantic Ocean with temperatures up to 125 degrees Fahrenheit in the summer months and only down to 65 degrees in the winter season, God could not have chosen a more idyllic place for me to live; I was ecstatic. And my love for meeting new people and Rhetoric and Writing would be utilized in that setting as Pastor of two churches in the southern part of the Island.

But God always sneaks in a little challenge so we won't become too comfortable and stop developing the fruits of His Spirit within us. You know what I mean: love, joy, peace, patience, kindness, goodness, faithfulness, gentleness and self-control. When I knew that I eventually would be traveling to live in some other country, I had asked the Lord to please not send me to Alaska even though it is part of the United States. My older sister, Mary, had married an Alaskan and they lived there for many years. She worked among the Eskimos and the Athabascan Native Americans near Fairbanks. She had asked me to join them there. Not one for cold weather, that was one of the last places on earth I would have wanted to live, even if it was to serve the Lord. As soon as I asked the Lord to, *"Please do not send me there,"* I immediately felt convicted and repented. Then He spoke to my heart that He would never send me to cold climates; instead, it would always be to warm, sunny locales. God is faithful to His promises and even though He sent me to Russia and England and Slovakia, the weather was unusually warm without fog, snow or cloudy skies while I was there which included weeks and months. Praise the Lord!

There I was on Isla de Gran Canaria, as the island is called in Spanish, sitting on my balcony terrace immersed in watching the storm, the streaks of lightning over the moonlit ocean and enjoying the rumbling sounds of the thunder. Then it struck me how much I missed the good, ole fashioned Oklahoma thunderstorm. There was a lump in my throat for the loneliness of what I was encountering, but in an uncanny way, I began to sense the presence of the Lord. The nostalgia of the sights and sounds became like a song, like melodies God was singing to me. He cocooned me with His love and His love was represented in His gift of the storm. This gift was greatly enhanced by the full moon reflecting upon the ocean's surface. The moon's light was so bright that I could see the streaks of rain pouring down. All sounds of the night, the crickets, the owls and other birds, were orchestrated by God to serenade me with His melodies. That is how it was.

Several years ago, the memories of that night flooded back into my thoughts as they often have from time to time. The prompting of God's Spirit came to me to write *"the blessing moment"* down and that is how the Title poem and this book *Midnight Melodies* came to be. All of the free-verse poetry was birthed through either my own experiences, the experiences of those whom I counseled in ministry or they were birthed entirely through the inspiration of God's Holy Spirit.

Within the Subtitle are the words *"Seas"* and *"Rivers."* My heart's desire is to convey Life in all its glorious colors and depths. *"Seas"* represent for me a connotation of the larger challenges that we, as the human race, face throughout the years we are granted to live. Those *"Sea"* situations will be huge, but they may be either of the calm, happy variety, or those with a few ripples, or some huge along with raging waves of turmoil, difficulties, even great sadness. They are usually the once in a lifetime events. Some of my poetical writings convey these *"Sea"* challenges. Then the word *"Rivers"* is suggestive to me of the smaller, narrower, daily situations of living. They may have their twists and turns, but they won't necessarily produce any overwhelming shock waves unless several circumstances meld together and cause a flood. In the totality of my poems, I hope I've conveyed the need and the joy of including God in all of the *"Seas and Rivers"* of our lives.

It is my prayer that you would read through the pages of this book, enjoy it, cry with it, laugh with it and let the Spirit of God speak to you through it. May God bless you for taking the risk to read it!

Your Servant, Rae Neal

Psalm 24:1-2

"The earth is the Lord's,
And all it contains, The world,
And those who dwell in it.
For He has founded it upon the seas,
And established it upon the rivers." NASB

Midnight Melodies

In the solitude of the night,
The dark night, the midnight hour,
God's midnight melodies begin to play.

The tide of the ocean below
Rushes in like choir waves on the sand,
Rhythmic voices, undulating voices,
Rising loudly, crashing, quietly receding.
His melody builds and ebbs
To announce the moon's rise
Arcing in the black sky,
A sky salted with sparkling diamonds.
The ocean's melody plays on,
Running the scale, higher and higher,
And back down the keyboard again.

In the distance an owl asks, "Who?"
And a cricket chirps its response.
Proud to make itself known,
Its melody plays like a violin;
Vibrating strings, loud and raspy.
Punctuated by the owl's hoots
Sounding like a didgeridoo,
They play in perfect harmony.

Suddenly Heaven's Conductor
Throws a lightning bolt down;
The drum roll of a summer storm
Breaks through while drops of rain
Begin to strike the window panes.
Like a harpsichord, the raindrops play
Their age-old familiar melody.
But soon the orchestral battle grows

As the bass drum adds drama
And thunders in the midnight melodies.

Night birds enter the arrangement
And rejoice in the refreshing waterfall
As if twittering their gratitude to God.
A crescendo reaches the climax
Of the night's rolling serenade.
So the midnight melodies play on
Until each note fades and falls
As if to say adieu to the hearer.
The drum beat ceases first when it's
A rumbling thunder in the distance.
Then the rain slows to a drizzle
And its gentleness is barely discerned.
The owl converses no more,
So the crickets need not respond.

Only the voices of the deep are heard;
Their own midnight melodies play on.
Then God brings the daylight's dawn
And the orchestra changes musicians
Until the hectic day closes its hours
And brings relief at the midnight hour,
In God's midnight melodies once again.

Psalm 42:7-8, *"Deep calls unto deep at the noise of Your waterspouts: all Your waves and Your billows are gone over me. ⁸Yet the Lord will command His lovingkindness in the daytime, and in the night, His song shall be with me, and my prayer unto the God of my life."* NKJV

A CUP OF WATER

Water pours refreshingly
From a cup in the hand of the Lord.
Drink deeply and be filled;
Quench your thirst as if the last sip.
Do you feel the power build within?
It's a supernatural liquid
Drawn from the spigot of eternity.
It is held in God's possession
Only for a chosen few.
Accept His offer to restore you
And be numbered among them.
There is no other stream that satisfies,
That nurtures, that stabilizes, that heals.
Once you have tasted
From His unending supply,
You will no longer desire the flow
From the earth's tainted wells.
Those wells spark no life
Give no fuel, sustain no soul.
Those wells tear away your dreams,
Eat away the flesh
And spring forth death.
They leave nothing but a forever dark,
A lost cry through a closed veil.
Choose wisely, child, and open your heart;
Receive the lavish stream that saves,
That splashes forth from His cup of love
And live forever with Him, with me.

John 4:14, [Jesus said], *"...but whoever drinks of the water that I shall give him will never thirst. But the water that I shall give him will become in him a fountain of water springing up into everlasting life."* NKJV

Revelation 22:17, *"And the Spirit and the bride say, "Come!" And let him who hears say, "Come!" And let him who thirsts come. And whoever desires, let him take the water of life freely."* NKJV

A Life, Dance

Dance, whirling
Goes the cadence of a life.
Spinning, turning
Go the years of God's dear child.
Jump, leaping
Over the moments, as all the days run by.

Play, singing,
Rising higher through the din.
Laughing, crying,
Spilling only the joyful tears.
Touch, kissing
Life's gift, a baby's soft cheek.

Grasp, hugging
All the things wild and all the tame.
Stand, pointing
At leaps of faith, the acts of grace.
Drive, speeding,
Reach the moon and the stars beyond.

> Give, loving,
> Ride the waves of celestial winds;
> Climbing, rising,
> Wisdom holds through rippled currents
> Ever to learn the spirals of love,
> Lifting always toward heaven's sweet home.

Skipping, running,
The clock's ticking never stops.
Ringing, chiming,
The bells toll for one like me.
Speak, thanking,

Before it's too late, the God who gave
A life, dance. Didn't you know,
      It's all His dance?

Psalm 30:10-12, *"Hear, O Lord, and be gracious to me; O Lord, be Thou my helper. ¹¹Thou has turned for me my mourning into dancing; Thou has loosed my sackcloth and girded me with gladness; ¹²That my soul may sing praise to Thee and not be silent. O Lord my God, I will give thanks to Thee forever."* NASB

A Moment and a Day Forever

It is a solitary moment like this
When the heart yearns for a day past;
A day gone by never to be lived again.
A longing in the heart reaches once more
For a glimpse of the love
That shone so brightly that day.
Twas a love that spoke not speaking;
Of acceptance given yet not requested;
A love that confirmed the truth
Though it contained the imperfect,
But did not condemn.
Instead, love became a fully opened rose
Suspended so sweetly between.
Oh, the confidence that love bestowed
With a name softly spoken,
The caress of a hand gently given.
No dimming of the eyes
Could ever dim its memory;
The passage of time could not erode it.
The memory, so lovingly kept,
So stubbornly cherished
Cannot but continue to live;
Death cannot creep into the thought
Of such a love as it was.
For it to have existed at all is inexplicable.

How does a moment's hello
Develop and expand into many years?
Those blissful years which slipped by
Without a thought, without awareness
Of how they soon would be lost;
Hellos and embraces never to be regained.
Count the marital bed

Among the greatest of losses;
Not ever to be filled with mirth again.
Yet, love recognized could not turn away;
The mundane would have been unbearable.
Better to grasp the memory of a day,
A moment God-given love was requited,
Than to let it go forever...
Forever.

Proverbs 18:22, *"He who finds a wife finds a good thing, And obtains favor from the Lord."* NASB
Ephesians 5:22, 25, 33, *"Wives, submit yourselves unto your own husbands, as unto the Lord...*^{25}*Husbands, love your wives, even as Christ also loved the church, and gave himself for it...*^{33}*Nevertheless, let every one of you in particular so love his wife even as himself; and the wife see that she reverence her husband."* KJV
2 Samuel 11:26, *"And when the wife of Uriah heard that Uriah her husband was dead, she mourned for her husband."* KJV

ANOTHER DAY TO FEED THE WORLD

Enchanted by the forested landscape
Shimmering in the dawn's light,
The inspired soul is accessed
To soar into the new day's challenge.

Morning birds chirp their way
From tree branch to flower petals
And herald delight for the new morning;
Heavenly gifts, vibrating colors of life.

Awaken sun child and stretch your arms,
Yawn to embrace the new dawn;
You, who paints landscapes with words,
Who drives the tune of faith and love
Like a dagger into hungry hearts.

Heed the calling of a fresh hour's path
And take your place on the pilgrim's road.
Wisdom from above is pouring down—
Catch it.
Smell the scent of His sweet love—
Breathe it in.
Open to the glimpse of heaven—
Envision it.

With silent erupting joy,
Allow the river to flow
Into life's sacred passage
Of God's merciful presence.
Join your heart with His purpose
To pull in the essence of divine words;
Fill up the reservoir to pour out,
Rescue the day with His love.

It's another day to feed the world,
Those hungering for His message.
Arise and go forth you sent one
To feed the world with His grace.

John 20:21, *"Jesus therefore said to them again, 'Peace be with you; as the Father has sent Me, I also send you.'"* NASB

Matthew 10:27, [Jesus said], *"What I tell you in darkness, that speak in light: and what you hear in the ear, that preach upon the housetops."* NKJV

A Trip To The Beach

Alone on the beach of a remote island
In the core of the southern Pacific,
I am languorously reposing
On these soft, white sands
That stretch as far as my eyes can see
To contemplate the serenity of this peaceful day.

The unblemished aqua of the heaven above me
Hovers so near,
If an arm were extended,
The hand might pierce it.
The intensity of the sun's rays
Dancing on the waters,
Reflecting on the sands,
Penetrates into every pore of my being.
The warmth bathes me
And bids me to stillness.
My spirit floats
And unites with the surrounding microcosm,
Enfolding me into its bosom.
A calmness and tranquility,
Such as I have rarely known,
Spreads through the core of my soul.
Quiet dreaming is disturbed
Only by the thunder of crashing waves
Pounding on protruding rocks nearby.

Being concealed from the masses
And nourished by the elements,
A courage I thought was lost
Is renewing, increasing, building
Upon the vigor and power
Of the ocean before me.

Glancing at its majesty, the undulating swells,
There is a stirring deep within me.
Submerged mysteries tug at my soul
Inviting, calling, even demanding
I explore their vast depths.

Finally, shaken out of lassitude,
I collect the snorkeling gear
That had been waiting beside me
And prepare for the trek
Into the adventure of the emerald sea
That beckons me;
There to discover God's handiwork
And all the variety His visions spawned.

It is always worth a trip to the beach;
To leave with a new heart song
And a praise toward God for all
His underwater beauties.

Isaiah 42:10, *"Sing unto the Lord a new song, and His praise from the end of the earth, you who go down to the sea, and all that is therein: the isles, and the inhabitants thereof."* KJV

BAKED IN YOUR LOVE

There is a hunger deep inside
That calls for love from only One.
Shove me into Your oven, Lord,
Bake me in the light of Your love.
Turn the heat of Your Spirit up,
Move the dial to the highest temp
To melt me with luscious joy,
And cause my soul to sizzle.
Take me from lukewarm, Lord,
And set me on fire for You
Until I jump, and shout and
Throw my hands into the air
To praise and worship with joy.
Finally, then I'll be satisfied,
Full to spilling over, but never
With my hunger ever stilled;
O, to be baked fully in Your love.

Luke 6:21, *"Blessed are you who hunger now, for you shall be satisfied. Blessed are you who weep now, for you shall laugh."* NASB
1 Peter 4:13, *"But rejoice, inasmuch as you are partakers of Christ's sufferings; that, when His glory shall be revealed, you may be glad also with exceeding joy."* NKJV

BLESSED WHISPERS

The jackhammer starts its rat-a-tat-tat
And even though a rooster's crow
Is never heard in the city these days,
The dogs still bark,
Car horns still honk,
And the dumpster clangs
And the garbage truck whines
As it mashes and squishes and grinds;
All determined to interrupt a daybreak's dream
And snatch away slow awakening to the sunrise.

Music is playing everywhere you go;
Office buildings, hamburger joints,
Department stores, the doctor's office
And the dentist's office, too,
(which might be a wise idea there).
You would think that hospitals would pipe it
To all its captive residents if it's so soothing,
But, no, there you must tolerate the intercom
Blaring out code blues,
Calling doctors to hurriedly respond.

The cacophony of sounds is so distracting
Competing for one's attention;
The squawk of a car's blaring radio
When pulled alongside, windows opened
While you await the too long pause
For a red traffic light to switch to green.
Dining in a restaurant, elegant with linen cloths;
The low din of voices is incessant
And drowns any attempts to converse
In voices of normal range and leaves you empty
Of romantic, candlelight's promise.

Midnight Melodies

A barrage of thoughts can be louder inside
Than sounds that assault from the outside.
Worry robs the night with its agitations.
"Could-have-dones," "would-have-dones,"
And the "should-have-dones" drone on
With the tick-tock of the clock stalling sleep.
A train's whistle in the distance
Draws forth a melancholy memory,
A jet engine roars overhead
And beckons your mind toward yearnings
To escape for a peaceful, holiday respite.

At last,
When all sounds fade
Into the silence of the night,
From somewhere between
Earth's bed and heaven's throne,
Whispers come in a dream;
"My peace give I unto you."
Blessed peace, blessed whispers.

John 16:33, [Jesus said], "*These things I have spoken unto you that in Me You might have peace. In the world you shall have tribulation: but be of good cheer; I have overcome the world.*" NKJV

CALL TO BATTLE

Drums beat in the distance
A trumpet sounds the reveille.
Arise triumphant soldier;
Throw on your armor,
Hoist your sword to your shoulder,
And mount your horse;
It's a call to battle.
Make the call rise spirit to spirit
To strengthen your power together.
With believers joined in agreement,
Shout forth the truth without error,
Stand firm upon unwavering ground.

Leap back into the ancient days,
Rescue the prophet, the seer, too.
They have been buried far too long.
We need a resurrection
Of God's revelations.
Give them their voices
For this new fresh generation.
Discern the spirit with spiritual sight,
It will take you to an unseen realm
Where gifts are open and on display.
Reach out and take one,
Then tell of a future day
Or make clear the present hour.
Bring the prophet to the front,
Stand him high upon a hill,
There he will send words to war
And drive the demons away.

Gather around them the armies;
Prepare to march into battle.

Make certain they are girded about
In such a way as to hold to truth;
Allow no darts to penetrate.
There's a detailed map God made,
Just follow closely His battle plan.
The King of Glory will ride ahead
And lead His people to victory.

Then all will be well
When we enter the fray
As we acknowledge
His call to battle.

Psalm 24:8, *"Who is this King of glory? The Lord strong and mighty, the Lord mighty in battle."* KJV
Zechariah 14:3, *"Then shall the Lord go forth, and fight against those nations, as when He fought in the day of battle."* KJV

CANTALOUPE

Cut open a cantaloupe,
Scoop out the seeds within.
How like my heart it seems;
Full of seeds unsprouted.
Take me back to childhood
Let the time start over.
Dream again little one,
This chance make it count.
Selfish grows; so shut it down
Selfless knows; it's a better plan.
Plant well this time and pour on water.
Nurture every tug of the heart strings
For the inner person knows
It's best to keep the dreams planted
Until they are fully ripe.
When next you look
There's a garden there;
And not one cantaloupe grows
But a whole garden full,
Which makes for a lifetime full.

Genesis 8:22, *"While the earth remains, Seedtime and harvest, And cold and heat, And summer and winter, And day and night shall not cease."* NASB

COLORS OF LIFE

Yellow, the sun rises upon a new life.
Green, the grass provides a child with play.
Gold, the eternal beckons and one commits.
Red, the heart beats for a teenage love.
Violet, the career spawns with a diploma.
Blue, the sky parts for parenthood blessings.
Brown, the nest empties with jumbled feelings.
Purple, the wisdom appears with approaching age.
Gray, the retirement from toil commences.
Orange, the fire of the sunset lowers.
Pink, the haze of light grows dimmer.
Black, the shadow of death takes the elder.

The colors of life have rounded the wheel.
Hues and blends have mixed the course.
But purity completes through the passage gate
And shimmering white will be its reward.

White, the believer is lifted into heaven,
Granted to make it their home forevermore,
And the color of true life begins just there
Where they shall be clothed in pure, white linen
To worship forever, Him on a white throne;
He Whose hair is white like wool,
He Who planned all those colors of life.

Revelation 3:4b-5a, Jesus said, "...*and they shall walk with me in white: for they are worthy.* *5aHe who overcomes, the same shall be clothed in white raiment...*" NKJV
Revelation 1:14, "*His [Jesus Christ's] head and His hairs were white like wool, as white as snow; and His eyes were as flame of fire:*" KJV
Revelation 20:11a, "*And I saw a great white throne, and Him Who sat on it...*" NKJV

COME UP HIGH

Climb up high and perch upon this platform
Where the birds fly high and the sky is close.
Survey the panoramic view before you
With your legs dangling over life's edge
And tell me what you see.
Your perspective must be different
Since you're not down to earth's level.

Down there you see only in front of you,
Nothing distant; just the crowds of a city
Like trees close by, a dense populace.
They amass on street corners at red lights
And nary a word is spoken in a greeting.
Vacant eyes on deadpan faces await a light
That governs whether they stop or proceed;
It is just another ordinary hesitation
To string out passages of a boring day.

Below, the air is heavy and hard to breathe.
Here and there an awkward glance betrays
A life without purpose or even a future plan.
Few voices are heard but when they speak
There's irritation, impatience and rudeness.
The tone of a voice exposes frustration,
Anger and despair becomes an expletive
As they escape the lips of one jostled;
Someone broke the invisible barrier
Deliberately set by an annoyed loner.
Distorted facial expressions abound;
The knitted brow, focused and intent
Contemplating life's endless obligations
With frustration and discontent.

Laughter is stifled in the street scenes below,
Not even a whisper or a nod of hello
Acknowledges a stranger who is passing by.
The tempo of footsteps is hurried;
They scurry and scuttle, dash and dart,
Marking a cadence for advancing masses.
Who can guess where everyone is going;
They are too close to see, too distant to know.

Come up high where all is peaceful,
Away from angry voices and frowning faces.
Come up high where the air is fresh,
And the view is clear and a destination is seen;
Where the brilliant pattern for a life's plan
Is laid out in all its magnificent colors.
The pace is slowed with time to ponder,
To breathe a prayer and seek for counsel.
An invitation comes from one Who matters;
It's the height and view of God, your planner.

Isaiah 55:8-9, "'For My thoughts are not your thoughts, Nor are your ways My ways,' says the Lord. ⁹For as the heavens are higher than the earth, So are My ways higher than your ways, And My thoughts than your thoughts.'" NKJV

Luke 2:14, "Glory to God in the highest, And on earth peace, good will toward men!" NKJV

CRAZY LOVE

Have you heard about a crazy love,
A radical love that shuns the mediocre?
It accepts nothing ordinary;
The common would be out of place.
That wild love reaches high
And stretches wide
The mind, the heart, the desires.
It expects the extraordinary,
The miraculous, the divine.
So pure and real does it display,
So penetrating and somber
Does its gaze behold;
The depths of the heart are explored,
Exposed, laid bare for the lover to see.
Motives are pulled to the surface
With nothing hidden from its view.
There's nowhere to hide, no desire to run,
No hesitation for momentary reflection;
Only abandonment to freely advance
Toward the direction of the crazy love,
Because it absolves, it sweeps away
And leaves no smudges, no hints
Of unfulfilled life left behind.
It opens up a clean board
On which to write a new story.
In response to the gentle pull
Of the promise that beckons;
The hungered life stretches,
And reaches and claims
The one Who offers
With outstretched hands
To take you to the light
Where all is known

And accepted and loved;
It's His crazy love,
It's God's love.

Jeremiah 31:3, *"The Lord hath appeared of old unto me, saying, Yea, I have loved thee with an everlasting love: therefore with lovingkindness have I drawn thee."* KJV
Ephesians 5:1-2, *"Therefore be imitators of God as beloved children; ²and walk in love, just as Christ also loved you, and gave Himself up for us, an offering and a sacrifice to God as a fragrant aroma."* NASB

DARK SHADOWS

Standing in the dark shadows of your life
She cannot be seen, she cannot be heard.
The words she speaks flow to the edge
But go neither beyond nor anywhere,
Certainly not into your hearing.
They hover there and finally fall,
Trapped in the darkness,
Dropped into deafness.
Poignant words they are, seeking their mark;
But wrapped in sorrow, in desperation
For a backward glance, a connection of sight.
But who can see into the shadows? Not you!
Obscurity is blindness to your exercise of will.

The chosen one, who seeks to be significant,
Is the woman protruding into your spotlight
Vying always for your exclusive attention;
She will speak and be seen and be heard.
Her sounds can be so deafening,
Drowning out the ignored and unperceived.

So you turn your deaf ear once again
To the one you neglect; she is weeping,
It is her, the one in the dark shadows.

Her cry, a prayer, flows up to the heavens
Where there is only One Who rescues.
Her broken heart lies bare, exposed,
In need of great and intricate repair.
Come forth, Holy One, in mercy spare
The wife standing in the dark shadows.

Proverbs 27:8, *"Like a bird that wanders from her nest, So is a man who wanders from his home."* NASB

Luke 4:18-19, [Jesus said] *"The Spirit of the Lord is upon me, Because He has anointed Me to preach the gospel to the poor. He has sent Me to heal the brokenhearted, To preach deliverance to the captives And recovery of sight to the blind, To set at liberty those who are oppressed, ¹⁹To preach the acceptable year of the Lord."* NKJV

Discovery of God's Designs

Leaping over the safe and secure boundary
Into the hazy unseen and unknown,
The courageous explorer dares to go.
The desire to know compels
So the door opens for the seeker.
The promise of enlightenment beyond,
Envisioned only by the searcher,
Beckons his forward momentum.
What might be gained?
What might be revealed?
What might be discovered?
Will the hunger to know be fulfilled?
Questions, spinning around in his thoughts,
Seek for answers to emerge from shadows,
To appear like the sun peeps through a cloud.
It's a trek not for the weak in character
Nor the fearful, nor the lazy or satisfied.
Discovery tugs on the courage of a willing heart
And lies across a great chasm from the sheltered,
From those too timid to venture across boundaries.

A strong desire calls out to the explorer
To investigate, to uncover, to expose the unseen;
Go by foot, take a ship, take to flight;
Peer through a microscope or a telescope;
Push through jungles, step on the moon,
Look inward, reach outward, gaze upward.
Mystery, mystery, lurks in the darkness
Clothed by shrouds of gossamer veils.
Only those who seek in Creation for Creation
Receive its invitation to travel on the quest
To reach through the unknown,
To journey for the thrill of knowledge

Through the dragons of the seas,
Through the demons of the heavens
And discover what only God has designed.

Psalm 40:5, *"Many, O Lord my God, are Thy wonderful works which Thou hast done, and Thy thoughts which are to usward: they cannot be reckoned up in order unto Thee: if I would declare and speak of them, they are more than can be numbered."* KJV

Dreaming

It is so lovely to lie supine upon a chaise
With lidded eyes drooping, half-closed, fluttering
As a dream presses and pushes for clarity.
Though the day is opening, why rise just yet?
No, let the dream play on as it floats into view,
Once more.

The warmth of morning sunshine caresses skin,
Gently nudging a reluctant body to awaken.
One hand leisurely reaches and pushes "play"
For music to softly accompany the reverie.
No, sweet dreaming, do not fade or recede,
Come back, again.

Oh, my, it's so easy to curl up and snuggle up
Sliding beneath the womb of a plump duvet;
It feels so cozy and warm, safe and secure.
The droning of a car's engine passes by and
Prompts a dog's barking in the distance.
No, not yet, and the dream drifts into focus
Coming back, yet again.

It is only a dream to be a person you are not;
To live in an abode not yours,
To live the life of a flamboyant character,
Who neither acts like nor resembles you.
Your purpose is so obscured in its context
You know this is not a God-given dream;
It is merely a fantasy.

Rise up, you visionary one,
Daybreak has burst forth and
Stolen your dreaming away.
Time for dreams to remain dreams;
What was hidden in darkened hours,
Spinning through your colorful mind
Must be discerned in the morning,
With the dawning light of a new day;
A day when it is expedient to put aside
All that is vain in dreaming.

Jeremiah 29:8-9, *"For thus says the Lord of hosts, the God of Israel: Do not let your prophets and your diviners who are in your midst deceive you, nor listen to your dreams which you cause to be dreamed. ⁹For they prophesy falsely to you in My name; I have not sent them, says the Lord."* NKJV

Dreams Don't Die

Dreams come in the night seasons.
They whirl around, materialize visually;
The stage sets, props plunk down
And once characters appear in place,
The curtain rises to reveal dream's story.

The script presents the vivid, in-color image
While the players move about and contribute.
Taking center stage, the picture focuses on you.
The action begins: you move to an easel.
With flare you draw lines with a pencil and ruler.
With precise dimensions girders are drawn,
Rising high upon a deep, cement foundation.
Step by step escape stairs are etched into place
Connecting floor after floor rising toward the sky.
Atop the edifice you place a pyramid-shaped cone,
It's diamond point pointing to the heavens.
After all, the dream and its inspiration
Comes from the one Who sits on His throne;
His heavenly royal home is far beyond your site.

Whether one acknowledges Him or not,
He is the Master Architect of design and form.
You have so ardently admired those mountains
Which loom nearby your developing edifice.
Then you recognize they are the Creator's design
And have become the towering pattern
For the beauty of your design now drawn.

What a blessing has been granted to you
To create and build in the character of God;
Visualizing and executing every tiny detail.
Is not your goal to please the discriminating eye

And make function the duty of your design
With all its grand scheme to meet the needs
Of those who will occupy and live within it?
In the universe of your structure reaching so high,
I'm sure you have imagined everyone in love
As they behold the fulfillment of your design
Because you have executed it so diligently.
Will they thank you and laud you with praises?
Maybe your name will not be known or recognized
And you will live as the creator in obscurity.
Even in that, you may be more like our Creator
Than you could realize when first you dreamed.

When you awake from your slumber at daybreak,
Will you take the risk and build that dream
By following after the image of your Creator
To never allow a dream to die?
If so, then you know dreams don't die
When you believe in God's creative power.

Laid out before you in the story of Joseph
You read that he dreamed a dream in Genesis.
Though years passed in captivity and labor
Even leading to the confines of a prison,
By the maneuvers of the hand of God,
There came a time of prosperity and honor.
In just the right time and perfect location,
The dream broke open and his family was saved.
They bowed down before Joseph in gratitude
And learned for themselves dreams don't die.

Take heart, you heavenly-minded dreamer;
When God gives forth a story in a dream,
Move forward in faith since you can know
That the story of dreams do come true.

Genesis 41:25, 32: *"And Joseph said unto Pharaoh, 'The dream of Pharaoh is one: God hath shewed Pharaoh what He is about to do.' ...^{32}And for that the dream was doubled unto Pharaoh twice; it is because the thing is established by God, and God will shortly bring it to pass."* KJV

Daniel 7:1, 13-14: *"In the first year of Belshazzar king of Babylon, Daniel had a dream and visions of his head upon his bed: then he wrote the dream and told the sum of the matters. ...^{13}I saw in the night visions, and, behold, one like the Son of man came with the clouds of heaven, and came to the Ancient of days, and they brought Him near before Him. ^{14}And there was given Him dominion, and glory, and a kingdom, that all people, nations, and languages, should serve Him: His dominion is an everlasting dominion, which shall not pass away, and His kingdom that which shall not be destroyed."* KJV

Flashes of Parenthood

Grand events,
Breathtaking moments;
So fleetingly they come, they vanish
Like the strums of a guitar's strings,
They vibrate strongly, then go silent,
But the notes linger on in your heart.

Children, blessings of God
Are blessed of God
When time is marked and recorded,
Written in the book of memories
Accompanied with images of love.

Grand events mark childhood years:
When a newborn baby's cry
Greets and punctuates its new world
With the startling discovery of a
Breathtaking moment;
When tentative glances of a first grader
Betray the challenges of climbing:
The first step up at the school bus doors;
Over barriers of making new friends;
Up the rungs of personal achievements;
The bridges to awards and recognition;
To a hope filled journey of brilliance,
Passing exams with honors;
Such are the flashes of parenthood.

All of a sudden a car's engine revs,
Behind the wheel is your teenager.
Concerns now exceed the past:
Of a bandaged, bloody, scraped knee;
Of a jump into the pool's deep end;

Of a tough tackle on the football field;
Of the first class for tae-kwon-do;
Minor breathtaking moments compared
To relinquishing control of the keys.

Enter your prom queen daughter
Dazzling in beauty, gowned in glory;
Her escort catches his breath
Upon sight of her allure and charm,
You catch yours;
It's a breathtaking moment.

A cap and gown implies a graduate,
A major step of accomplishment;
Each step down the arena's aisle
Leads to a breathtaking moment;
With a handshake, a diploma
A hat tossed into the air,
The world opens a giant door
And flings an array of choices
Into the arena of your child's heart.

Hope has accompanied every step,
A stairway to memorized moments.
Though only flashes in time,
The events are etched and recorded
Like an edited film which runs
Only when the switch is turned on;
The flashes of parenthood for sure,
Will always take your breath away.

Imagine how God,
Every child's Father, must feel.

Psalm 127:3-5, *"Behold, children are a heritage from the Lord, The fruit of the womb is His reward. ⁴Like arrows in the hand of a warrior, So are the children of one's youth. ⁵Happy is the man who has his quiver full of them; They shall not be ashamed, But shall speak with their enemies in the gate."* NKJV

Fools Go Down

Laughing clouds float above
And peer down upon absurdities of man.
Singing birds circle over heads of the haughty,
Waterfalls crash into the midst of man's leisure.
Light dances among opened flowers
Even as man's darkness threatens their closure.
Flights of angels dare to come near
Attempting whispers of peace in deafened ears.
The cry of His spirit invites all;
Drink in the water, true life is here.
Absorb the warmth of the eastern sun,
Take hold of the lifeline thrown your way.
Still, humanity's sea swallows the call of God.
Ghosts of the deep speak out,
Turn back, turn back,
Follow not the drownings of all the lost souls.
But around and around spins man's folly;
Laughter escaping when there should be tears,
Grasping for freedom when they should let go
And open for true wisdom that only God gives.
At the end of days, time has not waited
And the choices of fools go down, go down;
And the fools go down, go down.

Psalm 53:1, *"The fool has said in his heart, 'There is no God.' Corrupt are they and have done abominable iniquity: there is none that do good."* NKJV
1 Peter 2:15, *"For so is the will of God, that with well doing you may put to silence the ignorance of foolish men:"* NKJV

Footsteps in Front of Me

There was a time
When sunlight shone among the shadows.
What a relief to view what was revealed;
The beauty of a vision, a calling granted
To give one's life purpose and a legacy;
A significant plan to take one far away
To speak to others of saving grace
And a love so grand it lasts for eternity.
But *"how"* was the burning question,
How does one travel a life from here to there?

Then there were footsteps in front of me
And a voice spoke and feet appeared,
"Watch my feet and I'll show you the way."
It was a commanding voice, yet soft.
There was no mistaking its authority;
Experience cascaded within it
And exuded a love so profound,
It was assurance. It was the Lord.
His feet must be noted, so grand were they,
Not a blemish could be noted
And they shimmered with light.
One foot moved forward in slow motion;
A step forward, full of grace, the heel first
Then rocking past the arch up to the toes;
Every facet of progression spoke of more,
How one step was more than one action.
Ah, so natural, so fluid, it flowed
From each orchestrated muscle and tendon
Stretching, reaching to cover its distance.
One whole step with its every nuance
Gave onward momentum to advance;
The other foot lifted already in transition
Gave evidence there are many in one.

Whatever one accomplishes in life,
It seems to need a step by step process.
But His feet revealed that each step
Is never just one singular motion;
One part of God's plan leads to another,
Then to another as it comes to fruition.
Each form of witness leads to a witness
Each one in the middle of His calling.
My life's purpose fulfilled must be led
Following His footsteps in front of me.
They reveal that each part of the vision
Is its own fulfillment of the mission,
And just as important as reaching it.

Psalm 37:23, *"The steps of a good man are ordered by the Lord: and He delights in his way."* NKJV
1 Peter 2:21, *"For even hereunto were you called: because Christ also suffered for us, leaving us an example, that you should follow His steps."* NKJV
Acts 1:8, *"But you shall receive power, after that the Holy Ghost is come upon you: and you shall be witnesses unto Me both in Jerusalem, and in all Judea, and in Samaria, and unto the uttermost part of the earth."* NKJV

FRIENDS TOGETHER

You take my hand and stroll with me;
We take a walk through life together.
Mind to mind we think,
Word by word we speak,
Heart to heart our feelings collide.
Side by side we look to the future.
From time to time we backward glance
To see the distance traveled
And count what time has passed;
When darkness came, the power of deception,
When light shone bright, breaking its evil;
Remorse, the tears; a new course, the cheers,
The valleys raised and pride brought low.
Even now a glance, a tweak of the cheek,
Reassures the other is near.
Blessed repose when Christ bestows
A friendship that so interlaces.
Two hearts entwined, arms enwrapped
The best to support each other;
Because we are friends together.

John 15:13, *"Greater love has no man than this, that a man lay down his life for his friends."* NKJV

Gentlemen, Come Blow Your Trumpets

Come! Grab your trumpets American gentlemen
And blow your alarms for the days that are lost.
Gone are the days when a thirsty beggar
Could approach and knock on an unlocked door
To wait for the home's mistress to fearlessly inquire,
"What do you have need of, sir?"
"I'll sharpen a knife or a pair of scissors
For a drink of water and a bite to eat, please ma'am."
Willing to accommodate, she would find a dull knife,
Fetch the cup and add a peanut butter sandwich.
She served the fare on the family's daily China
And accompanied it with a homemade dill pickle.
She cared not about germs from his grimy fingers
Believing hot soapy suds would wash them away.
The offering was quickly consumed
As he leaned on the porch-steps railing.
Polite conversation would ensue
While he fulfilled his bargain with her
Until a satisfied smile would cross his face
And he would utter his grateful words,
"Thank you, ma'am. Good-day, ma'am."
Then he would be on his way;
His worldly possessions wrapped neatly in a cloth
Tied to a pole and hoisted onto a shoulder.
Soon he would disappear down the street
Leaving her wondering where next he would go.

When did the children walk or skip safely to school?
Gone are those days, too, when a bicycle rider
Could pump his way a few blocks to the school yard
To abandon his pride and joy in a niche of the bike-rack
Without a care for a thief's sight to covet and steal.

Later, the end-of-the-day school bell would ring,
And signal the student to mount his wheels again
To race his pals to the corner candy store
Where only a penny would purchase a treat.
Then it would be off to the corner park to teeter or swing
And chase his friends in a hide-and-seek game
Without fear of anyone lurking in the shadows
Harboring malice in their hearts with intent to harm.
The sun drooped lower and lower in the western sky.
The shadows of the youngsters grew longer
Than their short little bodies could fill.
Almost in response to their tummy's pangs,
A mother's voice would call out in the distance,
"Come home, son! Dinner is ready!"
Their carefree hours ended another day.
Slowly he biked home, pedaling past the streetlights.
Finally, the bike was left standing in the front yard
With its kickstand pushed to the ground.
Throughout the night, all was safe, all were secure.

What about the days when you could walk to town
And head back home with an armload of groceries?
Gone are those days when a passerby would stop,
Get out of their car to open a door and offer a ride.
Thankful for the long walk's interruption,
You could climb into the back seat without a thought
That you didn't know the name of the kind driver;
Just a helpful citizen who saw a need, you reasoned.

When on a short trip to a relative's home
In a neighboring town only an hour away,
It was common to see a sedan pulled over,
Parked along the highway with a flattened tire.
With a raise of the driver's hand calling for help,
You would stop and give aid to the stranded;

Usually a ride into town where the flat was fixed
Or a new tire was purchased and inflated.
It was okay to leave him there and be on your way,
Because another kind soul would return the driver
And help mount the new tire, just as a favor.
Long gone are the days when a hiker could point a thumb
And feel confident to hitch a ride whenever offered a lift
That no-one was looking for a naïve and trusting loner
Whom they could violate; whom they could murder;
Whom they could rape or even kidnap for a ransom.

Hurry, gentlemen, come blow your trumpets,
Sound the alarms to alert the people
That we have lost the days without fear.
We have lost the days when honor and trust
Were America's gifts to all mankind;
When kindnesses were common each and every day.
Yes, gentlemen, come blow your trumpets!
But, wait, where are the gentlemen?
Are there any gentlemen? Sound the alarms
And call the people to prayer; God, please help!

Joel 2:1, *"Blow ye the trumpet in Zion, and sound an alarm in my holy mountain: let all the inhabitants of the land tremble: for the day of the Lord cometh, for it is nigh at hand:"* KJV

II Timothy 3:1-5, *"This know also, that in the last days perilous times shall come. ²For men shall be lovers of their own selves, covetous, boasters, proud, blasphemers, disobedient to parents, unthankful, unholy, ³Without natural affection, trucebreakers, false accusers, incontinent, fierce, despisers of those that are good, ⁴Traitors, heady, highminded, lovers of pleasures more than lovers of God; ⁵Having a form of godliness, but denying the power thereof: from such turn away."* KJV

God's Breath

Hoorays and Hallelujahs! Thank you, God,
For Your breath that was a long time coming.
Perhaps it flowed from Your throne
Down through the ages
Passing through the Hill of Mars
Where Paul recited Your Spirit's calls.
Amid the ruins; not yet ruins,
Where great thinkers
Of Your wisdom and philosophy
Walked with their sandal clad feet,
Your breath absorbed the best of them
And was sent forward through time
To another future day.

As it hesitated in the English countryside,
It surely gathered the mores and customs
Of that regal country's era
Before it traveled forward
To a new land's coast.
The Puritans beckoned Your breath to linger
And join them for awhile for posterity
Before that day in 1776
Would call forth its final destination.
O happy day, blessed day
Came the 4th of July in that landmark year.
Come Saint Paul, come Martin Luther,
And you come, too, John Hancock,
And see what you have spawned.
Celebrate the gift of life
The Father breathed out and gave back then;
For on this day in 1776,
One nation under God was born.

Isaiah 42:5-9, "*Thus says God the Lord, Who created the heavens and stretched them out, Who spread for the earth and that which comes from it, Who gives breath to the people on it, And spirit to those who walk on it: [6]'I, the Lord, have called You in righteousness, And will hold Your hand; I will keep You and give You as a covenant to the people, As a light to the Gentiles, [7]To open blind eyes, To bring out prisoners from the prison, Those who sit in darkness from the prison house. [8]I am the Lord, that is My name; And My glory I will not give to another, Nor My praise to graven images. [9]Behold the former things have come to pass, And new things I declare; Before they spring forth I tell you of them.'"* NKJV

Gotta Walk the Cair Someday

Gotta see, gotta walk the Cair someday,
A friend's Oklahoma, country oasis
But minus the chiggers, the scorpions
And the creeping snakes, please.
Will have to pray God wraps me up
In a tight cocoon of His protection
To cover my body and eyes, for sure;
I don't want to view those creatures.
Just let me bask in the warm sunshine,
Feast my eyes on the rolling hills,
And listen to the rustle of the tall trees
As a summer's gentle breeze floats by.
Let me smell the wild-grasses aroma
And the perfume of the daisies nearby.
Let me stroll by the water's edge
Of the rain-filled pond which
Quenches the thirst of every fowl
That alights and dips its pointed beak.
I've heard it's a tranquil respite, Lord,
Created by You for Your children
To romp and play and chase the geese
And throw a line with a worm attached
In the hope of snagging a little fish.
Let me be such a child again, Lord,
Just to throw my cares into Your hand
And to once more love the wonder
Of exploring the wide-open spaces.
I'd delight to traipse through denser woods
And step from rock to rock in creek's bed.
It surely would be a pleasant day,
A day to restore, revive and refresh.
Bless God's hands for this created retreat,
An oasis from the world's daily crush.
Yes, gotta see, gotta walk the Cair someday.

Matthew 7:11, *"If ye then, being evil, know how to give good gifts unto your children, how much more shall your Father which is in heaven give good things to them that ask Him?"* KJV

Gratitude

Is it time to open the umbrella?
The rain is streaking upon my face.
With eyes squinting, His grace is falling;
The drink for a parched earth,
A soothing gift for my soul.
God is still moving in the heavens
With His sign of bulging clouds
To refresh the earth and the longing soul
And a provision is born for gratitude.

It's raining and raining and raining.
I can open up to be filled up
Again and again and again.
How generous is the Spirit of God
To orchestrate the heavens above
To saturate both the dusty earth
And the dried up soul below.
Seeds will grow and begin to mature
To blossom with lushness of gratitude.

No, best to keep the umbrella closed;
The better to receive and drink it in,
The beneficence of poured out grace
Spilling freely upon the ground;
The created earth and my molded heart.
So caring is the heavenly Gardener,
So loving is His nourishment
That the heavens, the earth and my soul
Are filled with the fruit of gratitude.

Acts 14:17, "...and yet He did not leave Himself without witness, in that He did good and gave you rains from heaven and fruitful seasons, satisfying your hearts with food and gladness."

Heaven's Music

Extrinsic, romantic, dreamy;
Let the music transcend the ordinary,
Take you soaring through the heavenly dome.
Violins, vibrate your strings;
Resonate with heaven's song.
Ivories and ebonies, run the gamut
From lows to highs
And carry your listener with you.
Steel strings, pick your way
Through life's melancholy strains
And challenge the reeds that blow with the wind
To reach the heights of the crashing crescendos.

Ecstasy, ethereal delight;
Let the music take you into its flight.
Leave the humdrum behind
And pass beyond the planet;
Yonder is no noise, no chatter, no screams.
Triangle ping, harp ripple with constant hums,
And golden trumpet, do alert and call all
To a triumphant spirit for rest at last.
Peace is held in the arms of the rhythm
Softly, gently swaying, lifting your hearer
Ever closer to the One Who sings,
"Come into My embrace and let the music be."

2 Samuel 6:5, *"And David and all the house of Israel played before the Lord on all manner of instruments made of fir wood, even on harps, and on psalteries, and on timbrels, and on cornets, and on cymbals."* KJV
2 Chronicles 7:6, *"And the priests waited on their offices: the Levites also with instruments of musick of the Lord, which David the king had made to praise the Lord, because His mercy endureth for ever, when*

Midnight Melodies

David praised by their ministry; and the priests sounded trumpets before them, and all Israel stood." KJV

Matthew 11:28-29, [Jesus said], *"Come to Me, all who are weary and heavy-laden, and I will give you rest. ^{29}Take My yoke upon you, and learn from Me, for I am gentle and humble in heart; and you shall find rest for your souls."* NASB

HE IS LIFE

He is life, massive life, tiny life, all life.
He is thoroughly and only life.
You can hear Him in a whispering leaf,
In the roar of a tornadic wind,
A baby's laugh, a bird's chirp,
The grounded fall of a tree,
The crack of a wallboard's snap
When the day's heat turns cold.

You can see Him in clouds rising high;
Rounded, cotton-candy white, then
Boiling, roiling, heavy dark lowering
Until split open, bursting forth rain.
It is not nature that is Him to worship,
But He is heard, seen, sensed in nature.
Hear the sounds that are His,
The morning roosters, moaning cows,
Costa Rican parrots soaring overhead,
Ocean waves slamming boulders,
Rocks hitting rocks
Bouncing down a mountainside.
A bee buzzes, a fish flips the lake-top,
All sounds are His, from Him, by Him.
Can't you hear the Creator in His Creation?

You can smell the water that is His;
Fresh rain, dewdrops, salty ocean, fishy river.
See the earth that is His;
Towering mountains, hot and sandy deserts,
Yellow sunrises, orange sunsets,
Blue lakes, muddy lakes, slimy lakes,
The beautiful, the ugly,
If you measure such things.

You can feel Him when you caress a baby,
Run your fingers over smooth marble,
Blades of grass and the rough bark of a tree.
How soothing to sense Him
When summer's heat penetrates the skin
And an ice cube brings relief to a burn.
He is in both, the hot and the cold;
How dare we prefer one over the other.

Children know His touch
When stomping in a mud puddle
And running their fingers through sand.
They are never in a hurry to escape the rain
Nor run from patting the coats of creatures.
When they touch, they feel,
When they look, they see,
When they listen, they hear,
When they hug and kiss,
They know God is there
And they know He is life,
Massive life, tiny life, all life.

Isaiah 37:16, *"O Lord of hosts, God of Israel, Who dwells between the cherubims, You are the God, even You alone, of all the kingdoms of the earth: You have made heaven and earth."* KJV

Psalm 139:7-10, *"Where can I go from Thy Spirit? Or where can I flee from Thy Presence? ⁸If I ascend to heaven, Thou art there; If I make my bed in Sheol, behold, Thou art there. ⁹If I take the wings of the dawn, If I dwell in the remotest part of the sea, ¹⁰Even there Thy hand will lead me, And Thy right hand will lay hold of me."* NASB

HER GREAT LOVE

She was a white-haired wonder;
Her long tendrils swept back
Twisted into a loose bun;
Untidy wisps floated in the air.
A gently swaying porch swing
Was an oasis of peace and gentleness
While she was sitting in its middle
As the evening sun disappeared.

Gentle, soft, quiet-spoken words
Uttered from her lips to child's ears
Sounded like love floating, encircling;
They swaddled each granddaughter,
One at her side and one on the other.
She could never tell them apart,
These twins of her daughter's;
They didn't know this,
She called both of them *"dear."*

Jesus, the name most often upon her lips
Was the guest in every conversation;
So real was this invisible visitor
Each *"dear"* believed He was there,
More so than Santa and Peter Rabbit.
She told riveting stories about Him,
This great love of hers,
With only a sprinkling of words.
Her story was told more in her manner,
Her face alit with the light of joy;
Not just a picture one remembers,
But a sensing deep in the heart
Of the truth of that pure love;
The sparkle in her eyes,

The warmth in her voice
Filled the whole world
For her daughter's twins.

Who's to say how one drops into a heart
And stays there through numerous years.
But these twins learned how and why
When one day Grandma's great love
Became the love of their own.
Jesus was Grandma's legacy to them,
A legacy of love that remains forever.

Matthew 22:37-38, *"Jesus said unto him, 'Thou shalt love the Lord thy God with all thy heart, and with all thy soul, and with all thy mind. [38]And the second is like unto it. Thou shalt love thy neighbor as thyself.'"* KJV

His Bride

The long-awaited moment has arrived.
The bride, gowned in dazzling white
Has begun her slow walk down the aisle.
Step by deliberate step,
She glides toward her Beloved.
Captured by her beauty,
The Groom appears transfixed.
Nothing exists for Him in the universe;
Only she is seen through His intense gaze.
Her heart leaps when she notices
And becomes acutely aware of His smile.
So full of admiration and longing,
His twinkling eyes draw her forward.
The culmination of love's glow
Has led to this spectacular moment
When all else fades from view
But for Him standing there
Waiting in anticipation
To take her hand in His.
For an eternity full of promise,
Her steps slightly quicken.
She lifts her head in regal fashion
Knowing she commands His attention.
Music of the heavens vibrates
And curls it way around this bride's head,
Setting the cadence for her every step
And wrapping the atmosphere
With tones of the majestic scene.
Though ages lent their years
Toward this day planned so long ago,
The youth and vibrancy of love's first glow
Is portrayed in the expressions of both;
The bride excited to receive His blessings,

The groom exalted as King to bless
And together they will reign forever.
Joined as one, their love will live
And give and bless throughout eternity.
The exquisite bride, adorned in the beauty
Of purity, of holiness, of desire to serve Him,
Shall be His, forever His bride.

Joel 2:16, *"Gather the people, sanctify the congregation, Assemble the elders, Gather the children and the nursing infants. Let the Bridegroom come out of His room And the Bride out of her bridal chamber."* NASB

His Voice Calls

There is a voice sweeping through the nation,
It's driving through borders and barriers,
Looking for attentive minds and open hearts.
It's winding around and between God's people
And seeks to wrap the lost in its summons.
The tentacles of the voice call out like a web
Attempting a rescue to bring sinners to shore.
On America's shorelines are amassed God's own,
They stand ready to retrieve and receive penitents,
Whether it's a church, a school, a grocery store,
Wherever life's shore of destiny positions you.
Hear the voice and heed its urgency,
O, you wayward and neglectful people;
You neglect the womb of its sacred mission
Yet give life to your mission of unnaturalness,
You allow the profane to enter your homes
And embrace the prurient and avoid the prudent,
You swindle your neighbor and call it justice
Groping always to satiate your appetite
When you hunger for more, ever to be enticed;
Swept away by your senses to touch and see.
Your body contorts in motions
Normally seen only by monkeys.
Maybe you desire to imitate them
Since you claim them for your ancestors.

Hearken to the voice when it comes to you,
Much is at stake; a citizenry is drowning,
Swamped by selfishness, an unholy greed.
The bell is cracked, there is no real liberty;
It's been shammed, scammed and swindled
By a definition distorted, never intended.
Listen to the voice that is beseeching you,

"Repent, repent, submit your errant will
To be redeemed, renewed and redirected,"
Then perhaps mercy will be granted,
Your country prevented from collapse
That is surely imminent otherwise.
The darkness that would cover the land
Because of your mindless rejection
Of God's truth and honor and love
Just might be averted and judgment lifted.
Listen, His voice is calling.

Joel 2:11-14, *"And the Lord shall utter his voice before his army: for His camp is very great: for He is strong that executeth his word: for the day of the Lord is great and very terrible; and who can abide it? ¹²Therefore also now, saith the Lord, Turn ye even to me with all your heart, and with fasting, and with weeping, and with mourning: ¹³And rend your heart, and not your garments, and turn unto the Lord your God: for He is gracious and merciful, slow to anger, and of great kindness, and repenteth Him of the evil. ¹⁴Who knoweth if He will return and repent, and leave a blessing behind Him..."* KJV

IMAGINATIONS

Mired down in the mind of imaginations
It's easy to get stuck on a web of suspicion.
It stretches out before you a scenario of lies
That feeds insecurity and starves the reality.
Truth falls trapped within its nest of vipers
That swallows every word of reassurance.

Can faith survive the assault of thoughts
That press into the heart for attention;
Those false pictures given reign
Spawned by jealousy, avarice and control?
Or is it swallowed up by its enemy of unbelief
That steals, rebukes and nullifies what's real?

Caution, O tormented one;
Don't slip through trapped doors beneath
And slide into the darkness that awaits.
It will void your life with emptiness
And leave no mark upon your soul
But arrows pierced into life's blood
With no rescue from the false left in sight.
Untangle and release yourself;
Dump those vain imaginings of betrayal,
And broken promises and tragedies.
Yield your mind to the only light there is
And allow truth's invasion to return,
Harness your thoughts and bring you freedom.

The power of God's Word is strong
And will cast self's ugly vanity away.
It will lift you up out of death's spiral
To live and see the light of truth once more.

II Corinthians 10:3-5, *"For though we walk in the flesh, we do not war after the flesh: ⁴For the weapons of our warfare are not carnal, but mighty through God to the pulling down of strong holds; ⁵Casting down imaginations and every high thing that exalts itself against the knowledge of God, and bringing into captivity every thought to the obedience of Christ;"* NKJV

Romans 12:2-3, *"And be not conformed to this world: but be transformed by the renewing of your mind, that you may prove what is that good, and acceptable, and perfect will of God. ³For I say, through the grace given unto me, to every man that is among you, not to think of himself more highly than he ought to think; but to think soberly, according as God has dealt to every man the measure of faith."* NKJV

IN THE TWILIGHT

In the twilight, the evening's dimming light,
The paced seconds crawl toward stillness,
Moments seem to slide down ever slower.
Each breath suspends it pace
And hovers between activity and slumber.

The quiet becomes full of unnoticed sounds;
You can almost hear music in the trees
As tree branches sing with their leaves.
The gentle thumping of one's heart
Synchronizes with the ticking of a clock.

In the twilight, shadows stretch out long,
The fading light fights their encroachments.
The approach of darkness brings clear focus;
Thoughts not heard, speak loudly and invade
With an acuteness of self-emergence.

The resonance of a voice seems to thunder;
Words strongly hang in space in the silent air,
And plead next for gentle whispers instead.
The pace of the day is in slow motion
Like time has run out of minutes.

Inhale, exhale, even breaths can be heard.
Each passing moment is acute, real, touchable.
A numbing inertia overtakes arms, legs;
Just to sink onto a porch swing is an effort.
Yet thoughts come gently, now turned inward.

In the twilight, the evening's darkening light,
A still small voice filters in through the haze;
"You are mine now," He says, "come to me.

Let me soothe the day's cares away,
Give you peace and lavish love upon you."

So the God who made you, is finally heard.
Not in the hustle of the busy day,
Not amid the noises of competing voices
Nor honking horns or ringing phones,
Only at day's end, in the hush of the twilight.

1 Kings 19:11-12, *"And He said, Go forth, and stand upon the mount before the Lord. And, behold, the Lord passed by, and a great and strong wind rent the mountains, and brake in pieces the rocks before the Lord; but the Lord was not in the wind: and after the wind an earthquake; but the Lord was not in the earthquake: ^{12}And after the earthquake a fire; but the Lord was not in the fire and after the fire a still small voice."* KJV

LEAVES

The leaves are swirling overhead,
Dancing on the winds.
Painted in shades of golds and reds,
They signal the exchange of warmth for cold.
The vibrancy of autumn leaves belies
The dormancy of what lies ahead.
One by one, they float to the ground
Where they lie until their colors fade
And the supple leaves become brittle.
As life transforms into death,
The nostalgic recall of vibrancy
Of the days that transpired behind
Causes lament for those brighter days
To languish in "what might have been"
And "what could have been."
With only bare branches looming ahead
And nothing left to declare beauty,
The song of the heart yearns
For the springtime of lost years;
The hope that leaped in joy
With the thought of time's minutes
Stretching endlessly ahead.
Yet now when hope has slowed
And time's passages crawl along
Laboriously groping for another day,
The only fulfillment that opens ahead
Is when the skies part wide
And the spirit takes up
What lay in the shadow of death
And the cold of winter is no more.
The sun shines again,
New life bursts forth;
New colors transcend beyond

The colors of earth's limits.
The transition is completed,
But this time the leaves remain,
Never to drift downward again.
This time life's tree is forever
Because Christ has set its roots
And ordained its leaves to heal.

Revelation 2:7, [Jesus Christ said] *"He who has an ear, let him hear what the Spirit says to the churches. To him who overcomes, I will grant to eat of the tree of life, which is in the Paradise of God."* NASB

Revelation 22:1-2, *"And he showed me a river of the water of life, clear as crystal, coming from the throne of God and of the Lamb, ²In the middle of its street. And on either side of the river was the tree of life, bearing twelve kinds of fruit, yielding its fruit every month; and the leaves of the tree were for the healing of the nations."*

Left Behind

Forgotten are the times that creased the brow;
And sorrow punctuated every syllable spoken.
Gone are the days of melancholy strains;
When tears wet the cheeks and sobs pierced the quiet.
What could heal the gulf that seemed so wide
Between the despairing heart and a river of joy?

A gentle call in a soft voice
A tug on the heartstrings
Does turn seeking eyes upward
To search from whence the calling comes.
"Come to me," He urges,
"You who are so heavily laden;
And let me give you peace and rest,
Stop the hunger that so invades your heart
And occupies the thoughts of your searching mind.
The longing is for me, my love."

When once yielded to the words of promise,
A love so pure fills the expanse of emptiness;
The unidentified voice becomes known.
Only love from the Divine can lift a desperate soul
And rescue it from the precipice of life's ending.
What was not realized as lost is found
And the purpose of life is discovered;
To walk with, to talk with
The Creator of our flesh and spirit.
He becomes the joy of every moment
And all the heartaches and all the tears
Are left behind.

John 17:7-8, 26, *[Jesus said] "Now they have come to know that everything Thou hast given Me is from Thee; [8]for the words which Thou gavest*

Me I have given to them; and they received them, and truly understood that I came forth from Thee, and they believed that Thou didst send Me. ...²⁶ and I have made Thy name known to them, and will make it known; that the love wherewith Thou didst love me may be in them, and I in them." NASB

Revelation 7:17, *"for the Lamb in the center of the throne shall be their shepherd, and shall guide them to springs of the water of life; and God shall wipe every tear from their eyes."* NASB

Revelation 21:4, *"...and He shall wipe away every tear from their eyes; and there shall no longer be any death; there shall no longer be any mourning, or crying, or pain; the first things have passed away."* NASB

Light Side, Dark Side

Why would anyone fear the dark?
Did distortion of the dark occur?
Stories and movies abound
Creating fear out of the dark.
Dark in character lurks the evil
Dark in deed slinks the criminal
So both are cast in black;
Bad cowboys don black hats,
Good cowboys don white hats,
What an injustice has been done.

Out of the dark, light was birthed.
There is no way to know light
Without also knowing the dark.
There is much to contemplate
That there can be a bright, light side
To every dark side simultaneously.

A piano is made with ebony keys
Interspersed between the ivory keys;
Some are flats and some are sharps,
Yet using both makes music ethereal.

The earth turns on its axis;
Light slowly fades into dark;
The body reclines and relaxes,
Then the eyelids close to dream.
Night gives way again to the light,
The eyelids flutter open
And motion soon follows.
Wasn't the dark good for slumber?

Life begins in the dark.
It gestates from egg to fetus
And grows into a viable baby.
Out of the darkened chamber
A child is birthed into the light.
Though life forward
Has its own light side
And has its own dark side,
They can be intermittent
But usually are intermingled.
Who can say one benefits
A life more than the other?

Seeds are planted in the ground
Where germination takes place
In the secret place of the dark.
Soon the sprouts peek through,
They shoot up toward the light.
The seed that was planted,
Is not longer a seed,
But reveals itself in day's light,
Maybe a fruit, perhaps an onion.
How can the dark be ugly
When out comes nourishment?

One day life ebbs,
Dark swallows up the light;
Death drags the body to the grave.
Alas, the final light parts the dark,
Breaks open life from death's grip
And the power of resurrection
Has brought the light side
And broken the dark side forever.
Isn't it reassuring to know
That passing through the dark
Leads to the eternal light?

It must be the work of the devil,
The deceitful one's distortion
That preys upon man's thoughts
To equate the dark with evil
When the Creator gave us both
The light and the dark together.

Genesis 1:1-5, *"In the beginning God created the heavens and the earth. ²And the earth was formless and void, and darkness was over the surface of the deep; and the Spirit of God was moving over the surface of the waters. ³Then God said, 'Let there be light;' and there was light. ⁴And God saw that the light was good; and God separated the light from the darkness. ⁵And God called the light day, and the darkness He called night. And there was evening and there was morning, one day."* NASB

Love's First Bloom

When love's first bloom opened,
The beauty was breathtaking
And the perfume excited the senses.
The freshness of dazzling dewdrops
Added to each unfolding petal,
Heightened its regard and
Nourished each facet of reflection.

How love beckoned and drew the heart
To find in its embrace the warmth of touch.
Then heaven's challenge summoned
To make discovery a sweet surprise
That lay in wait behind each door.
The heart's chambers were unlocked;
With each whisper they opened
And laid bare their disclosures
Of hurts experienced and dreams dashed.
Confessions were offered
Acceptance given.
How vulnerable a place love gave
To expose one's depths of thought and deed
And plunge one beneath the hand of mercy.

Nevertheless, the heart entrusted
And believed
And desired;
The perfect union that absolved
That purified
That blessed
That nurtured.

It seemed that it would last
When love's first bloom opened;
But a flower's head droops,
Its brilliant beauty fades,
Petals fold and fall to the ground.

So love's first bloom must fade
To make room for a new garden;
One that flourishes in every color
Like gray days as well as sunlit days,
Days of autumn when some things wither,
Days like snowdrifts of winter's cold.

Days of springtime come again,
Faith and trust and hope maintain
A humble love, kind and generous.
When God's love is joined between two,
He makes and tightens a three-fold cord;
His grace and mercy tweaks heartstrings,
Love strengthens and refuses to break.
It grows then and thankfully matures
As God adds depth to enrich and replant
Love's very first bloom.

Ecclesiastes 4:11-12, *"Furthermore, if two lie down together they keep warm, but how can one be warm alone? [12] And if one can overpower him who is alone, two can resist him. A cord of three strands is not quickly torn apart."* NASB
1 Corinthians 13:13, *"But now abide faith, hope, love, these three; but the greatest of these is love."* NASB

Mirror, Mirror

Mirror, Mirror, who are you reflecting;
The young girl with long, blond pigtails?
She is so vivacious and precocious.
She lives for the moment,
Her friends and all the fun times.
She skips a rope and runs like the wind.
One day she walks down a lonely road
And sees her future in God's hands,
But the moment passed and
Off she went to live her life,
Her way.

Mirror, Mirror, who are you reflecting;
The young woman with a smooth coiffure?
She is so industrious and a bit audacious.
She lives for her future days
Always searching for a husband.
She works by day and dances at night.
One day she finds herself near death
And God's hands extended once more.
"Go back to your life and live for me,"
So she returned to earth to live His plan
His way, just for awhile.

Mirror, Mirror, who are you reflecting;
The wife and mother with frosted light hair?
She is so tenacious, but a lot pretentious.
She lives for the present;
Her country club friends, cocktail parties,
The two-story house and fancy cars,
And travelling to far away, exotic places.
She walks forth on the arm of her husband
Instead of leaning on the sure arm of God

Until one day, her mate was gone;
The arm she thought was so secure
Was now around another.
So she called on God and gave Him all,
This time the call went deep
So she went forward to live her life,
God's way.

Mirror, Mirror, who are you reflecting;
The daughter of God with her silver hair?
She is so studious and judicious;
With the Lord's love, she is luminous.
She lives still, her life isn't finished;
Her future embodied into the present.
One day God had come for a visit
And laid out before her His finest plan;
Trust in Him, one day at a time.
So all He promised is being fulfilled;
She lives a rich life,
It is all for Him.

Matthew 6:19-21, *"Do not lay up for yourselves treasures on earth, where moth and rust destroy and where thieves break in and steal:* [20]*But lay up for yourselves treasures in heaven, where neither moth nor rust destroys and where thieves do not break in and steal:* [21]*For where your treasure is, there your heart will be also."* NKJV

MYSTERY

Mystery, mystery, everywhere mystery.
Deposited into the minds of men,
Instruments of witty inventions.

Gaze into the heavens above,
Draw near the hidden orbs now visible.
Though their winding paths are declared,
Still mystery shrouds their origin;
From where descends you fiery one?
What icy path brought you, cool blue one?
Spinning, circling, speeding, arcing;
Wandering the vast and dark expanse
You travel your courses,
Destined for where; how came you?
Mystery, mystery, everywhere.

Peering down through glassy lens,
A tiny life becomes exposed;
Brought close and magnified,
The before invisible is now in view.
One cell, then two, now four and more,
Dividing the infinite life from one
Yet forming a solitary life from many;
The many are drawn, one to another
Attaching, absorbing, blending, growing;
What creature is this in the making?
Mystery, mystery, everywhere.

Amazing design, enthralling revelation;
Mysteries in the macrocosm veiled by night,
Mysteries in the microcosm veiled by light,
One by one the veils are split open
And knowledge replaces the unknown.

From whom comes this revelation?
Who tore the veils that we might see
Some mysteries are mysteries no more?
The maker of the inventions? No.
It is the one Who knew their designs,
The Designer of all, the God of all.
For Him there are no mysteries at all.

Proverbs 8:12, *"I, wisdom dwell with prudence, and find out knowledge of witty inventions."* KJV

Revelation 15:3, *"And they sing the song of Moses the servant of God, and the song of the Lamb, saying, Great and marvelous are Thy works, Lord God Almighty; just and true are Thy ways, Thou King of the saints."* KJV

Job 28:11-12; 23-24, *"He dams up the streams from flowing; And what is hidden he brings out to the light. ^{12}But where can wisdom be found? And where is the place of understanding?...^{23}God understands its way; And He knows its place. ^{24}For He looks to the ends of the earth, And sees everything under the heavens."* NASB

Revelation 10:7, *"But in the days of the voice of the seventh angel, when he shall begin to sound, the mystery of God should be finished, as he hath declared to his servants the prophets."* KJV

No More Good-Byes

In the cold, winter haze of an ice-foggy morning
I ventured out of my front door
Looking for the sun to warm the day
And bring cheer to a sad heart,
But it had disappeared.
Another day to have to reach inside
And somehow pull out the light
To accompany me through the hours just ahead.
It's one of those times
When nothing on the outside
Can contribute in aiding support
For the stretch of emotions
That lie ahead to say good-bye
To a long ago friend;
A friend not seen,
A friend not spoken with
In the long, intervening years.
Yet still in the thoughts
Tucked away under the label
Of innocent childhood memories,
Are moments shared of raucous laughter
While riding double on a bicycle;
Running the challenge of a 100-yard dash
Straining toward the finish line
Just to reach it before the other;
Memories of long serious chats
Over what to do and where to go
The next lazy day of summer;
Conversations over a party-line phone
With a thread-wrapped cord
And a rotary finger-dial, all in black.
Then came the day when bicycle
Was traded for a motor scooter

And a moment of maturity threatened.
I climbed aboard behind him
And gingerly placed my hands about his waist.
I remember the first-time feel of flesh
So pronounced through his thin t-shirt;
The amazement that came with that touch:
So this is the person I've run with
And laughed with and joked with.
He suddenly became so real;
This person was a real human being.
He had flesh that was warm;
He had a heart that beat
And I could feel it pulsing
As I wrapped my arms
So brazenly around his chest
And held on for dear life.
It was his manner to lean the scooter
While he careened around street corners.
Now his flesh is cold
And his heart is silenced.

Dear Lord, our lives are but a twinkle
In your eternal, all-seeing eyes.
Yet you entertained to think of him,
This childhood friend of mine.
You shaped him knowing these hands
Would one day touch his waist.
You blew into his nostrils
Giving him breath to laugh with
And a voice to speak with.
You fashioned his legs to run
And his hands to grip handlebars;
Youthful memories were birthed.

Thank you, Lord, for my dear friend;
Too soon gone for any good-byes.
On this foggy, chilly day, I look to You
To bring Your warmth of Sonlight
Upon the memories to be laid to rest
Along with my friend today,
Knowing both will join You
Until some day, we will laugh
And run and enjoy friendship again,
Where there will be
No more good-byes.

Psalm 139:14-16, *"I will praise Thee; for I am fearfully and wonderfully made: marvellous are Thy works; and that my soul knoweth right well. ^{15}My substance was not hid from Thee when I was made in secret and curiously wrought in the lowest parts of the earth. ^{16}Thine eyes did see my substance, yet being unperfect; and in Thy book all my members were written, which in continuance were fashioned, when as yet there was none of them."* KJV

II Corinthians 5:8, *"We are confident, I say, and willing rather to be absent from the body and to be present with the Lord."* KJV

No More Time

Racing, racing, time speeding;
Moment after moment
Melting into another,
Tripping, running away,
Stumbling, but sliding on,
On through the future days,
Since there is no brake.

Our souls lament
The passage of yesterday
And the far away years
In the distance behind.
There is no mechanism
To fall backward
To relive a single day;

So,
We strain against the sunset,
But light fades to shadows
And the night approaches still.
Gone are the youthful years,
Gone are the fruitful years,
The strong and energetic years;
They are challenged and defeated,
Faded from memory, taken by time.

The shades are pulled down,
The curtains drawn closed;
The soul enters the dark night
To pass into heaven's light.
Death collects the time
And returns it to God
Who had ordained it,

Recorded it, and granted it,
Until there is...no more time.

Revelation 10:5-6, *"And the angel which I saw stand upon the sea and upon the earth lifted up his hand to heaven, ⁶And sware by Him Who lives for ever and ever, Who created heaven, and the things that therein are, and the earth, and the things that therein are, and the sea, and the things which are therein, that there should be time no longer:"* NKJV

Ocean of Life

The ocean of life is there,
The choice is yours.
You can touch the surface,
The glasslike tranquility;
But the risk may be too great,
The ripples too disturbing.
Best perhaps to glide along,
Slipping past the memories;
The depths tears elicit,
The heights where laughter spills.
Let them all slip past you
Without a pause or a thought;
See, not know, be seen not known.
O, the bliss of anonymity,
Its pattern is undisturbed.
Gentler are the moments,
Brighter are the skies.
Because the sunlight disguises;
There are no storm clouds there.

Then there is the other choice,
That of the uncharted sea.
Break through its surface,
Gently push to the unexplored.
Let the downward lunge take you
Swimming to the depths below.
Dare to plunge into the eddy
Where there seems to be no light.
The stream of life hidden there
May take you through disturbances,
Through fissures of the heart
That bubble up and open wide.
The darkness may blind your view;

So you must extend your hand
And reach for God to find your way.
Awkward groping, gasping for breath;
Just what does it prove to you?

The treasures of the deep
Suddenly expose themselves
Through thoughts, through smiles,
Through tears, through kisses and hugs;
No strangers are here, all is laid bare.
The challenge gives forth its reward;
A love so vast, a love so deep
The treasures of the ocean become yours.
They are all found in the depths of life;
God, Himself, is our ocean of life.

Proverbs 8:17-21, *"I love them that love me; and those that seek me early shall find me. ^{18}Riches and honor are with me; yea, durable riches and righteousness. ^{19}My fruit is better than gold, yea, than find gold: and my revenue than choice silver. ^{20}I lead in the way of righteousness, in the midst of the paths of judgment: ^{21}That I may cause those that love me to inherit substance; and I will fill their treasures."* KJV

Ouch!

Ouch! The long thin branch
Removed from a pear tree limb
Smarted when it struck my legs.
That should teach me a lesson
To stop wallowing in the mud.
How dirty are my lovely white shoes!
They aren't fit to wear anywhere now
Especially to share the Good News.
My footprints would leave a dirty trail
And perhaps taint another friend's home.
Oh, my lovely Sunday School dress,
It's no longer clean and gleaming white;
Sadly, it's torn and hanging in shreds.
It should be scrubbed in a washing machine
To remove ugly spots with snow-white suds.
Since it's so terribly stained with muddy water,
Maybe it's better to exchange my garment.
Of course when I stomped in that mud puddle,
It splattered murky muck upon my face;
Now I can't see clearly to find my way;
Someone will have to guide me home.
Look at my fingers, how filthy they are!
Whatever I touch could definitely be ruined.
Best not to go where others may see me,
They might think I'm just a big brat
Who deserved the punishment given.

Please, hurry God, I know I did wrong;
I simply want to be clean again.
Forgive me, Lord, and hear my promise;
One thing is for sure, I am determined,
In all my future years, I will never
Ever jump into another mud puddle

Nor give cause to have to shout, "Ouch!"
Never, ever again.

Psalm 38:17-18, *"For I am ready to halt, and my sorrow is continually before me. ^{18}For I will declare mine iniquity; I will be sorry for my sin."* KJV

2 Corinthians 7:9-10a, *"Now I rejoice, not that you were made sorry, but that you sorrowed to repentance: for you were made sorry after a godly manner, that you might receive damage by us in nothing. ^{10a}For godly sorrow works repentance to salvation..."* NKJV

Ephesians 5:25b-27, *"...even as Christ also loved the church and gave Himself for it: ^{26}That He might sanctify and cleanse it with the washing of water by the Word, ^{27}That He might present it to Himself a glorious church, not having spot, or wrinkle, or any such thing; but that it should be holy and without blemish."* KJV

PLEASE

A word gently slips past her lips in a whisper;
The plea is spoken and begs,
"Please."
That one little word takes flight
And descends lightly upon the wings
Of a passing angel.
So aware of the urgency of her heart's cry,
At that moment, the angel accepts the burden
And lifts her care and carries it away.
Mindful of her critical need,
The angel streaks through the heavens
And like lightning,
Passes every threatening barrier.
Filled with tears and peppered with anguish,
A lifetime seems embedded within the little word,
The beseeching, urging word,
"Please."

The destination is in the far distance,
But in the twinkle of a moment,
The angel bears its cargo homeward.
Suddenly the enormous gates of heaven open,
The angel sweeps toward the golden throne.
A voice quietly booms from its glowing midst,
"What word is delivered unto Me this day?"
Gingerly landing in a respectful stance,
The angel brushes a wing with its hand,
Collects and cups the word on its fingers.
In a bow before the throne,
With head down and arms lifted high,
The word is presented;
Her small word is spoken in its whisper,
"Please."

Quickly the response came,
It, too, in a loving whisper,
"The answer is 'Yes,'
Be blessed, my child,
For your babe shall live this day."

Psalm 91:11, *"For He will give His angels charge concerning you, To guard you in all your ways."* NASB

Hebrews 1:14, *"Are they [angels] not all ministering spirits, sent out to render service for the sake of those who will inherit salvation?"* NASB

Matthew 7:11, [Jesus said], *"If you then, being evil, know how to give good gifts to your children, how much more shall your Father who is in heaven give what is good to those who ask Him!"* NASB

Practice

(In memory of my son, Lance, d. 1-22-2011)

It is said, *"Practice makes perfect."*
So I say, *"Thank you,"*
Even when I don't mean it.
Practice means pressing on the notes of life
When there seems to be no melody,
Only a monotonous drone, dull, simplistic;
It's all the same, no variation, all flat,
Nothing sharp, nothing clear; no focus.
Day after day, moment after moment;
Melding moments, so steel gray, so lacking,
Yet I move, take a step, wobble, another step;
Grateful for one, then another...really?
But where is the music, the song?

Keep going, practice the sequence:
Arise, say, *"Thank you,"*
Clothe, say, *"Thank you,"*
Swallow food, say, *"Thank you,"*
See, hear, speak and say, *"Thank you."*
Acknowledge the sun, though scorching;
Accept the rain, though drenching;
Address the cold, through shivering;
It's good, it's needed, it just is, the weather.
Say, *"Thank you."* Practice it, practice again.

Then the birds begin singing,
A train whistle blows, a car horn blares,
A cadence breaks through to the dulled mind.
A rhythm seems to develop without effort;
And it rises, billows up, circles around,
Calling for attention, for the listening ear;
"I'm here: the minutes, I'm here: the notes."

Little by wrenching little, the heart-freeze thaws.
Practice, practice some more; say, *"Thank you."*
Could there be an affirmation? Confirmation?
Feel the pain now, because it's real, death is real;
I say, *"Thank you,"* even for that.

Finally, then it comes, there it is;
Gratitude, thankfulness, true thanksgiving.
I can feel the Lord near
And a song bursts through.
To Him, I say, *"Thank you."*
It's no longer just practice!

I Thessalonians 5:18, *"In every thing give thanks: for this is the will of God in Christ Jesus concerning you."* KJV

QUESTION

Do the wild flowers still bloom
At the cattle guard, near the pond?
How like life they are;
In a fleeting moment,
They raise their budding heads,
Then they fall
Just at the height of their full beauty.
Few of them are hardy and persevere;
Most are so delicate and fragile
Their perfume fades and petals drop;
One by one, their beauty is forgotten.
If there is a memory,
It is a ghost of what was;
It doesn't match the fragrance of reality.
There's no lasting power in their heads;
Their glory droops, shrivels and dies
Leaving nothing behind, not even a hint
Of their time in the sun with intense colors.
Nodding in the breezes to greet, 'Hello,'
Too soon, their gentle waves say, 'Goodbye.'
Then they are gone, or are they?
That is the question.

One day, shoots push up through the dirt;
Their visible offspring burst forth.
The question has been answered.
How like life they are; their seeds live on
And once again, the wild flowers bloom
At the cattle guard, near the pond.

Zechariah 8:12, *"[Thus saith the Lord of hosts;] 'For the seed shall be prosperous; the vine shall give her fruit, and the ground shall give her increase, and the heavens shall give their dew; and I will cause the remnant of this people to possess all these things.'"* KJV

Release of a Saint

For freedom lovers across America
Who stand in the gap and pray,
Laud those saints who persevere
While they languish and suffer
In filthy prisons with unkempt floors
And little food to nourish their bellies
Much less their tortured souls,
Solely because they belong to Jesus.

Cry tears of remorse for every saint
Who has been chosen for courage
And its human demonstration
Of steadfast faith and open resolve
That the love of the Lord restrains
And secures their heart for Him.
Though shackled, their spirit is free.

Rejoice, Saints, and shout your praises
For the love of God meets the test;
Release is secured
And barred doors opened.
Through the sweet aroma
Of every tear and unrelenting prayer,
The enemy of God has acquiesced.

The evil is defeated once again
And the victory of the cross remains.
Saints, sing for joy and offer praise
For the release of our friend, Meriam,
Whose courageous stand
When death was in view
Deserves our honor and our tribute
For her brave and godly resolve!

She paid the price of discipleship;
Surely she has treasures in heaven!

2 Corinthians 4:8-11, *"We are troubled on every side, yet not distressed; we are perplexed, but not in despair; ⁹Persecuted, but not forsaken; cast down, but not destroyed; ¹⁰Always bearing about in the body the dying of the Lord Jesus, that the life also of Jesus might be made manifest in our body. ¹¹For we which live are always delivered unto death for Jesus sake, that the life also of Jesus might be made manifest in our mortal flesh."* KJV

Remember

O death, where is your door?
Remember, life is of God
      And He shuts you out.

O hate, how can you exist?
Remember, God has
      Overcoming love.

O anger, how much can you rage?
Remember, peace is the fruit of
      God's Holy Spirit.

O sadness, do you think
      You can extend the night?
Remember, His joy always
      Comes in the morning.

O envy, how intense
      Can your jealousy be?
Remember, God's purity
      Is surely pure as white.

O complaint, why your
      Condemnation?
Remember, God in earliest days
      Gave His assessment.

Death cannot obliterate the first day,
Hate was not a thought in mind.
Anger had no causative factor,
Sadness was empty from the heart.
Envy could seek nothing to gain,
There was no complaint to state

Among all created perfection.
It's expedient that you remember
You destroyers did not exist at all.
The first day led to the sixth day;
Everything God created was "good."

Genesis 1:10b, 12b, 18b, 21b, 25b, *"10b,...and God saw that it was good. 12b,...and God saw that it was good. 18b,...and God saw that it was good. 21b,...and God saw that it was good. 25b,...and God saw that it was good."* KJV

SPEAK

Speak to me now
Help me understand.
Speak a little louder,
I really can't hear you.
Lean closer in to me,
I still can't hear you.
Your mouth is open
And your lips are moving;
I just don't know why
It's so hard to hear you.

O, now I understand;
It is clear to me now
And so easy to hear you.
It's there in your eyes,
The pain that goes deep;
The words you couldn't speak,
You speak with silent screams.

Woe to the one
Whose pain overwhelms
And silences all emotions.

Concealed cries of heart hurts constrict
As they fill up your internal reservoir.
Threats of bursting must find escape
To release pent-up pressures within.

Let liquid drops begin their seepage,
Let them merge into a widening stream
Until the current so quickens its pace
It finally becomes a gushing torrent.
Where else can a raging flood flow

But through your two closed eye-lids.
You've long held them tightly shut
Like doors locked with a skeleton key.
A stricken will may prove to be fixed
But time forces barriers to crack.
When pressures build and threaten a split,
Fissures appear you cannot hold back;
Brokenness crashes right straight through
And demands heaven's attention.
It's the seat of love, so you can be certain
The cries of your heart are understood.
God will hear your gushing torrents,
And let them speak for you;
Then He will relieve you of your pains
And your silent screams will be vanquished.

Speak to me then,
It will be easy to hear you.

Psalm 61:1-2, *"Hear my cry, O God; Attend to my prayer. ²From the end of the earth I will cry to You, When my heart is overwhelmed; Lead me to the rock that is higher than I."* NKJV

Such a Name!

Such a cute, little pixie face,
With an adorable white stripe added;
It travels down the top of my nose,
Gives me a distinguishing demeanor.
No others in the whole wide world
Are adorned as gorgeous as I am.
If I sound prideful, it's truly deserved,
You may observe it in my slinking
As I sling my voluptuous hips.
Take note of my shiny black coat,
People remark that its fluffiness
Belies how adorable I appear.
I'm loved the most by chic ladies
Who understand my allure;
The tidy appearance of an arched tail
Designed like a feathery fan and
Displays the elegance of wide stripes.
I bear the color of my Creator,
The purity of white down my back.
There is one more trait, the envy of all;
I carry with me a most delicate perfume.
But jealousy of people can be so intense,
Many run away and malign my name.
I'm sure they just desire to smell
As deliciously wonderful as me.
If children had been taught as little tykes
How lovely and sweet is my perfume,
Then everyone would be my friend
And love how special I smell.
But envy betrayed adults' feelings
When they gave me such a silly name;
It doesn't describe me at all.
In fact, they did me a disservice

And they might have offended God
When they called me a *"skunk."*
How unflattering!
God created me different, unusual,
So unique with perfume attached.
My competition is the rose!
How dare Adam give me such a name;
It has no charm, aroma or spunk.
Call me Chanel, Dune or Breeze;
But never should it have been
Skunk!

Genesis 2:19, *"And out of the ground the Lord God formed every beast of the field, and every fowl of the air; and brought them unto Adam to see what he would call them: and whatsoever Adam called every living creature, that was the name thereof."* KJV

Swept Into Her Future

There she goes running down the street,
Her long red braids wound around her head.
Her black, baggy slacks have empty pockets,
So she stops long enough to request a dollar.
Her desperation is in her gulps for air
As she pants in shortened breaths.
Her parents have forsaken her
Dumped her, really, out into the world.
Sad girl, wanton of love and hungry
Calls for help in her own forlorn way;
A bite to eat, a place to rest, maybe a ride.
Guided by a hand unseen, hidden to the eye,
Another young woman who has fallen in love
Stops on the corner where the girl passes by.
History has caught them both in its grasp
And hurls down the highway of ancient days;
A splintered, wood cross plants between them
Tall and erect, dressed in red blood.
At once when confronted by the girl's request,
The woman, smitten with the joy of love
Offers her hand holding a crumpled dollar
And a word gently given, softly spoken
Intended to capture the frayed girl's notice;
"I have fallen in love and I will share Him, too.
He is the most generous one I ever knew,
I'm sure He will be happy to care for you."
The girl asked His name
And if He could spare a room.
With laughter the explanation poured out,
"His Name is Jesus. He has gifts for you,
More than you could ever dream. Come.
He will feed you and give you all you need.
Sit with me awhile; let me tell you of Him."

So history came alive on that street corner;
The girl with the baggy pants and red hair
Would learn of the cross and His great love
And be swept into her future that day.

John 6:35, *"And Jesus said unto them, 'I am the bread of life: he who comes to Me shall never hunger; and he who believes on Me shall never thirst.'"* NKJV

Take A Little Walk With Me

Take off your shoes, pull off your socks,
Come, take a little walk with me.
Step with bare feet upon the green cushion
Of lush, grassy lands that stretch over the hills,
Past the horizon, beyond what our eyes can see.
Watch the colorful birds in flight overhead,
How carefree they glide upon billows of air.
They artfully demonstrate their aerobatics,
Reaching the heights, and then spiraling downward;
In circular motions they dip their wings to greet us.
Vibrant pastels in the field of flowers ahead
Shimmer in every hue, showing off for me and you.
Slowly they raise their heads, some tiny, some massive,
And nod assent that we may roam among them.
Their sweet fragrances tickle our noses
When we pause to caress their soft petals.
So delicate and light are the flickering butterflies
When they alight upon our heads and our bare arms,
Their slight touch is barely noticeable, barely felt.
Graphic patterns are etched into their wings
That dwarf their tiny bodies when spread wide open.
The drone of the bees buzzing catches our attention,
So we watch them bob in up and down motions
As if the flowers' centers are their trampolines.
Intermittent sounds emit from the crocuses
An invitation for us to lie down in a carpet of clover,
As if to exclaim, "Summer days are here again,
Enjoy the symphonies of our concerts!"
A grasshopper jumps his long jump
And looks at me in askance with bulging eyes,
"Did I impress or shall I sprint again?"
Then off he goes to hop and hop and hop.
All of nature seems in perfect harmony

Like a synchronized band;
The sounds, the colors, the motions.
Surely it's a little bit of Heaven, a glimpse into the future
When all will be alive, You, me, every blade of grass,
Every insect, every animal, every flower;
Called by our magnificent Creator
To harmonize together in the light of His loveliness.

Genesis 1:12, 25, 30: "*[12]And the earth brought forth vegetation, plants yielding seed after their kind, and trees bearing fruit, with seed in them, after their kind; and God saw that it was good. [25]And God made the beasts of the earth after their kind, and the cattle after their kind, and everything that creeps on the ground after its kind; and God saw that it was good. [30][Then God said]...'and to every beast of the earth and to every bird of the sky and to every thing that moves on the earth which has life, I have given every green plant for food;' and it was so.*" NAS

Teardrops and Diamonds

One by one the teardrops fall;
They splash before the throne and pool.
Quickly now they become a sea,
As far as the teary eyes can see.
Scoop the tears up, dear Lord,
Catch them with Your upturned hands,
Let them trickle down Your loving arms.
Please, pat them upon Your tender face;
Feel the anguish submerged in the tears.
By Your power turn them into diamonds
And command the angels to disperse them.
Dispatch them back to their anguished owners
And place the jewels within their suffering hearts.
May the sparkle from Your love arrest their tears
And light the way again to joy.

Lamentations 2:18-19, *"Their heart cried unto the Lord, O wall of the daughter of Zion, let tears run down like a river day and night: give thyself no rest; let not the apple of thine eye cease. [19] Arise, cry out in the night: in the beginning of the watches pour out thine heart like water before the face of the Lord..."* KJV

Revelation 21:4-5, *"And God shall wipe away all tears from their eyes; and there shall be no more death, neither sorrow, nor crying, neither shall there be any more pain: for the former things are passed away. [5] And He that sat upon the throne said, 'Behold, I make all things new.' And He said unto me, 'Write: for these words are true and faithful.'"* KJV

The Creator's One-At-A-Time

Sitting in the balcony of a concert hall
With the orchestra center-stage below,
The music of an unknown composer
Drifted upward to fill my hearing
With melodies that transcended reality.
My spirit lifted into a dreamlike state
Of wonder and astonishment
Over the intricacies of notes and harmony.
A question arose through my drifting thoughts,
"How did anyone compose such stanzas of beauty?"
Then I heard God's still, small voice,
"I inspired one note at a time."

Relaxing one evening in a coffee house,
Surrounded by friends with beverages in hand,
An elderly woman with frosty hair
Was introduced and arose to the microphone.
During the next forty minutes,
I was transported to her home village
In a different country, of a different time,
To witness the ravages of world-wide war
And sense the terror of a small, trapped child.
"How could she speak of such pain and sorrow?"
Then came His compassionate voice,
"I encouraged her one word at a time."

Landing at New York's Kennedy airport
Was the fulfillment of a long-awaited goal.
Known as America's melting pot and the Big Apple
Could not prepare me for the skyscrapers ahead.
The taxi took the bridge across the East River,
Where crowded, cavernous avenues loomed into view
Shadowed by tall buildings rising to the heavens.

With flabbergasting amazement, I wondered aloud,
"How could man build such towering structures?"
God's voice explained, "In My image; he fulfills a vision,
One measurement, one stone and one day at a time!"

Gazing at a television screen with sleeping baby on my lap,
The dimly lit room enhanced the glaring moment.
It was a warm, summer night on July 20, 1968,
And the whole world waited for only one man.
Then the door opened on the lunar module,
The Eagle of the Apollo 11 spacecraft.
9:56pm, Central Daylight Time, Astronaut Neil Armstrong
Stepped his left foot onto the Moon's surface
Which he described as the "magnificent desolation."
"How had the dreams of science fiction come true?"
The Lord's voice revealed,
"I allowed man the 'one small step' at a time."

Driving one bright, sunshiny morning
In the country of Spain along a coastal highway,
I fought to steer around hairpin curves
And to keep the fear of heights at bay
As I traveled to the tops of steep mountains.
There were no guard rails there along the ledge,
Just a cliff side drop to the ocean foam below.
Two hours later I finally rounded a bend
That revealed a valley below full of yellow daffodils.
I gasped, "Who created such breathtaking sites?"
God's voice answered me, "I did, one day at a time."

Isaiah 46:18, *"For thus saith the Lord that created the heavens; God Himself that formed the earth and made it; He hath established it, He created it not in vain, He formed it to be inhabited: I am the Lord; and there is none else."* KJV

The Exchange

Breathing life into the world
So connects with our thoughts,
And flows out from the spirit.
What is the life?
Is it something stagnant, deadly,
Degrading, hindering to an upward flow?
Or is it something stirring, lifting,
Generating, motivating to reach its best?
If you are of the first mind,
There must be a renewal
That comes from an exchanged heart
Or what life there is will slowly kill
To leave death in its wake
With no breath left to give.

If you are of the second mind,
An exchange has already been attained
Or there could be no true life's flow.
There is unfiltered freedom and
Expression requires no censor,
Only beauty can flow from the spirit;
Colors from the paintbrush,
Words from the ink pen, or
Inspired utterances of the lips.
Your heart of chilling cold was exchanged
For your warm heart of radiating love
Breathing life into the world;
Sustained life, true life, it is God's life.
He Who made your exchange.

Mark 8:36-37, [Jesus asked] *"For what shall it profit a man, if he shall gain the whole world and lose his own soul? ^{37}Or what shall a man give in exchange for his soul?"* KJV

The False Accusation

Oh, the damage of the false accusation;
Cutting, slashing, ripping through
The deepest fabric of the soul.

Lying words have a life of their own
When levied against an innocent victim.
The accusation is bandied about and
Careens like a highway from mouth to ear,
And from mouth to ear, racing and weaving
Without caution or stop signs in their travels.
Oh, the glee with which the words are spoken;
The perpetrators nearly dance like puppets,
So eager are they to leap to the next listener.
The master of lies orchestrates their ballet
Making certain they drip their poison about;
Sometimes with whispers in private,
Sometimes with shouts in public
Until the whole of society is told
And the soul of the culture is shredded.

Yes, the words have a life of their own
When spat full of venom at the victim.
They spiral into the victim's ears
And race throughout their body
Attacking thoughts and sparking nerves
Until they reach deep into the heart,
The very core of the unsuspecting.
The words slam into the deepest recesses
Intent upon annihilation of the psyche,
Destruction of the personality and reputation
With irreversible damage to the emotions.
The false accusation hammers hard,
Unsatisfied until it squeezes the heart

And causes tears to squirt rivers openly
And the soul of the person is destroyed.

Oh, the master of manipulation
When first he manufactures the lie.
His plan is to tear apart a society
Through the destruction of every person.
He seeks for the willing participants
Who throw caution and investigation away,
Only to believe a false tale and spread it.
He seeks for the unsuspecting recipients
Who will allow entry of the accusation
And succumb to their soul's disturbance.
What can stop the court's tribunal?
Who can stop assassination of a soul?

Only Truth can halt a runaway lie.
If bearers of tales will seek the Truth,
They will discover Truth's Name is Jesus.
Jesus will present the way to stop the tongue
And restore the culture to wholeness.
Only Jesus can heal the broken-hearted
And restore the injured soul to soundness.
In the end, the enemy is destroyed,
And his lying mouth is shut;
The initiator of the false accusation.
He lies defeated at the bottom of the abyss.
He is defeated by Truth, by the Lord Himself
And Truth shall live in victory, forevermore.

Matthew 5:11-12, *"Blessed are you, when men shall revile you, and persecute you, and shall say all manner of evil against you falsely, for My sake. ^{12}Rejoice, and be exceeding glad: for great is your reward in heaven: for so persecuted they the prophets who were before you."* NKJV

Revelation 12:10, *"And I heard a loud voice saying in heaven, Now is come salvation, and strength, and the kingdom of our God, and the power of his Christ: for the accuser of our brethren is cast down, which accused them before our God day and night."* KJV

THE FREE RIDE

Sir, I see you have a new, red sports car.
It's a beauty with its convertible top down.
Would you please take me for a ride?
I love the drive down a two-lane highway
Where we can blaze by the fenced wheat fields
Waving golden in the summer's breeze.
It's lovely to pass beneath the leafy branches
Of age-old trees intertwined
Forming a tunnel above our heads.
It's so nice to speed up and down steep hills
That feel like the dips of a roller-coaster;
And to slow down for the curves
Shaped like Christmas ribbon candy,
Then head for the straightaway
And race the car's shadow
Until we pass in a blur
The cement creek bridges.
It's the feeling of the wind
Swirling through my hair,
It's the feeling of the sunlight
Beaming down upon my face,
It's the speeding down the highway
With no barriers in sight
That brings laughter from deep within.
I can lean my head back,
And stretch my arms straight up
Toward the heavens above,
Toward my loving Savior
And watch white, cottony clouds
Float through the baby blue;
Then comes that feeling of freedom.

Midnight Melodies

Racing down the highway
In a sports car open to the world
Without a burden or a care,
The joy of life floods my soul
And causes me to feel
Just the way God made me
To want to feel;
Free.

John 8:32, 36, *"And you shall know the truth and the truth shall make you free. ...³⁶If the Son therefore shall make you free, you shall be free indeed."* NKJV

THE JOY OF PAIN

(Dedicated to my son, David)

Pain, pain, searing pain, screaming pain;
Every cell vibrates with pain.
Pain, no chance to think,
Pain, no chance to breathe,
All is consumed within it.
Nothing else exists.
Hour after hour, the pain never ceases.
Moment by moment, the pain remains.
Second to second, the pain is intense.

Darkness gives way;
The sky parts. The pain fades.
O blessed interval of relief;
Light compels, my spirit soars
Toward the outstretched hand
And the peace that beckons.
But a voice is heard, "Go back, dear one,
There's work to do, a plan to fulfill.
Choose to come or choose to go,
It's up to you. You must decide.
All is possible, if willing to try.
You can do it, if you only believe.
Should you return, I will be there with you,
Then you will make it; you will go on through."

At once back, it all returns;

Pain, pain, searing pain, screaming pain,
My body writhes with pain.
What is this?
The cry of a babe is heard.

O what relief, free at last.
Hello, my son,
Blessed peace,
Blessed love,
Blessed joy.

Genesis 3:16, *"Unto the woman He said, I will greatly multiply thy sorrow and thy conception: in sorrow thou shalt bring forth children; and thy desire shall be to thy husband, and he shall rule over thee."* KJV

The Midnight Hour

The midnight hour is approaching,
Coming into view.
Our journey has almost ended;
The final minutes are just ahead.
Can we make it through the night,
Its darkest moments to endure?
The monsters fast approach
Snarling and gnashing their teeth.
Death looms nearby,
But there is no death.
The smell of smoke is in the air
But there is no fire.
The earth trembles
And the animals scream.
The stars are hidden
And the moon is blood-red.
There is no light,
Only dense, thick darkness.
Seek for a place of safety
A place wherein to hide,
The best to persevere
Until the breaking of the dawn.
Quietly sing a new song
Purposely in praise
Just to draw near
To the One who set the clock.
In His embrace is mercy
To encourage through time's end,
When blessed trumpet sounds
To herald the rising of the dawn.
Welcomed light shines brightly
To display the devastation
Of those lost to perdition.

But in daylight's splendor,
The One Who rides from the east
Mounted upon a white horse,
Stretches forth His hand
To sweep across the lands
And all is made new;
The midnight hour is finished.

1 Corinthians 15:51-53, *"Behold, I tell you a mystery; we shall not all sleep, but we shall all be changed, ^{52}in a moment, in the twinkling of an eye, at the last trumpet; for the trumpet will sound, and the dead will be raised imperishable, and we shall be changed. ^{53}For this perishable must put on the imperishable, and this mortal must put on immortality."* NASB

Matthew 24:35-36, Jesus said, *"Heaven and earth will pass away, but My words shall not pass away. ^{36}But of that day and hour no one knows, not even the angels of heaven, nor the Son, but the Father alone."* NASB

Isaiah 65:17, *"For behold, I create new heavens and a new earth; And the former things shall not be remembered or come to mind."'* NASB

The Smile of a Child

A twinkle of delight worth living for
That rescues from life's morass
Is a child's smile that lights up their face
And lights up your heart, as well.
Even better is when a giggle breaks forth
And their eyes shine and their bodies ripple
When it turns into unrestrained laughter.
Then simple joys become amplified
As memories from the past resurface
And pictures roll through your mind
Of long ago years and forgotten moments.

A recall from younger days is
When nothing else but the sunshine
And a tarnished blue bicycle
Make promises for a carefree afternoon.
Pedaling as fast as you can,
You're off to your best friend's home.
The wind blows in your face
And billows fill out your blouse.
The fake motor of the queen of spades
Attached to the rim with a clothespin,
Flaps on the spokes and alerts the neighbors
Of your passing by or pending arrival.

With a child's smile in front of you,
Another memory slides into view;
A summer evening with friends on the block
Chasing around the corner street-lamp.
The worthy mission for the entire gang;
Capturing fireflies as they twinkle by,
Coaxing them into pint-size canning jars
With lids poked through by an ice pick

To prevent their quick demise.
What odd creatures they are, we thought,
To carry flashlights upon their backs.

A child's smile is a cherished reminder
Of long ago days that lay behind
And the shortened days looming ahead.
A child's smile elicits your own,
Maybe even a giggle or two.
The smile becomes the curved loop
That links us all to eternity;
Parent-child, parent-child,
Until we come full circle
To God the Father and to His Son.
With their welcoming smiles
They lead us to our ancestors;
To parent-child, parent-child
And we become forever linked
Through the smile of a child.

Luke 18:16, *"But Jesus called them unto Him, and said, 'Suffer the little children to come unto me, and forbid them not: for of such is the kingdom of God.'"* KJV

THE THROES OF GRIEF

A shadow advanced and draped her heart
Until a wrenching lament escaped her lips.
It was filled with groans so intense,
A listener would wonder if death lurked near.
What foible of life, what wretched event
Could arrest such a young woman near forty
And stretch her cries to the point of breaking?
So listless was the raising of her hand,
When she made feeble attempts
To swipe the wet tendrils of her raven hair
From her tear-streaked face;
So bent was her lithe body
That she crumpled to the floor.
Abandoned to the discomfort there
Of the cold and hardened wood,
It matched the cold hardness of her despair.
Her soul fled into the darkness of grief,
Not even a glint of light could stream in.
A word of solace was not heard
So could not bring her any comfort.
The embrace of a loving arm
Was not acknowledged nor was it even felt.

Lying on the floor, near where she had stood,
Was a sheet of crushed paper which had floated,
Dropped from her hand to its resting place there
Only a few shocking moments before.
A letter. A confirmation. A condolence.
An official seal adorned its heading
Accompanied by a uniformed soldier.
KIA…Killed in action.
The fruit of her body,
The blood of her blood,

The bone of her bones,
The flesh of her flesh,
Now gone. Life gone. Future gone.
Nothing left but the throes of grief.
God help the Mother! No one else can.

Isaiah 53:4-5, *"Surely He [Jesus Christ] hath borne our griefs, and carried our sorrows: yet we did esteem Him stricken, smitten of God, and afflicted. ⁵But He was wounded for our transgressions, He was bruised for our iniquities: the chastisement of our peace was upon Him; and with His stripes we are healed."* KJV

THE UNKNOWN

Come along into the unknown.
Though it's a place where sight is nil;
Hardly a beginning is apparent
And no end can be discerned,
No walls or parameters designed,
The adventure is worth the trust.
Let courage muster for the first step
And let God carry you into a reaching,
Then the stretch will position you
For a filling up and a spilling over;
A tuning to His call of outward flow
Of expression's process of motion.
A surprise He has within the unknown
Becomes a wonder for all to know
And see and feel and experience.
Creativity has mastered past the dark
And materialized into the light.
Hooray for the bleak unknown
Where imagination and wisdom is free,
Becomes full and makes known
What was not imagined first by man
Nor thought
Nor planned
Nor seen.
It's the unknown where creation exists
And the force of the Creator is revealed.

Amos 3:7, *"Surely the Lord God does nothing Unless He reveals His secret counsel To His servants the prophets."* NASB
Amos 4:13, *"For, behold, He Who forms the mountains and creates the wind and declares to man what are His thoughts, He Who makes dawn into darkness and treads on the high places of the earth, The Lord God of hosts is His name."* NASB

THE WORD

Speak the word and touch my soul.
I hear it as it slides into my heart.
It's a powerful word, strong in depth
Reaching toward the ache deep inside.
It lives and makes alive what was dead.
Such a need there is for that one word;
All the world thirsts for it,
Cries out for it,
Hungers for its soothing embrace.
Its soft caress presses inward
And releases all my salty tears and yours;
Tears that have pierced like daggers,
Tears of anguish, tears of sorrow,
Tears of loss for the wasted years.
So much time lost in the throes of pride;
Never willing to let go, stiff-backed,
Full of desire never fulfilled,
Always looking inward but never seeing,
Weighted down with crushed hope,
Reaching but never grasping,
The harshness of self-will
Deceived, dragged down into a dark abyss.
There is only one way out;
That one word must be spoken,
It must be heard, accepted, believed,
Then all the garbage of a thrown-away life
Can be cast out and exchanged,
Renewed with its gracious gift.
The word calls and lasts;
It will never desert nor let go.
The soft word spoken ever so firmly
Impacts one soul, the world, the heavens;
That one word so carefully chosen,

So determined to reveal its power.
One word full of joy, dripping with love,
Never has there been such a word
More endearing, more freeing.
But it must be spoken by only One;
The One who defined it, envisioned it,
The only One Who can speak it,
The only One Who makes it vibrant,
Real, life-giving, eternal.
He is the only One Who wrote the word,
Who grants it, delivers it, applies it
And caresses your soul with it.
He is the Lord of heaven and earth,
The Creator of your bursting heart
That longs so agonizingly for Him
And His one word dripping with love.
He is your Savior and the word is
"Forgiven."

Luke 6:37, *"Judge not and you shall not be judged: condemn not, and you shall not be condemned; forgive and you shall be forgiven."* NKJV
Luke 7:47-48, *"Wherefore I say unto you, Her sins, which are many, are forgiven; for she loved much: but to whom little is forgiven, the same loves little. ⁴⁸And He said unto her, 'Your sins are forgiven.'"* NKJV

TRUTH WINS!

Zing! There went the probe,
I know it quite well.
The extraction was perfect
And presented in bare form.
What a thought it was
Wrapped up in deception!
An opinion, a supposition,
A theory, a conviction,
And don't leave out presumption;
Such words are thrown about
For correctness of supposed truth.
Yet they are only a language;
A dictionary thrown around
Couching truth with deception,
With betrayal, pretense and deceit.
When raised to the surface,
Placed under a microscope
With the light of examination,
The thought is dissected,
Scrutinized by the Holy Word.
Realization of gross trickery
Dumped by the deceiver
Unleashed a deep remorse.
All hail Holy Spirit's power,
He led to repentance door!
Such as the lying thought was,
It has been turned to advantage
With genuine wisdom replacing it
Leaving the structure of the mind
Bathed and washed clean.
Hallelujah! Truth wins!

Hebrews 4:12, *"For the word of God is quick and powerful, and sharper than any twoedged sword, piercing even to the dividing asunder of soul and spirit, and of the joints and marrow, and is a discerner of the thoughts and intents of the heart."* KJV

1 John 2:20-21, *"But you have an unction from the Holy One, and you know all things. [21] I have not written unto you because you know not the truth, but because you know it, and that no lie is of the truth."* NKJV

Voices of Martyrs

The voices of martyrs scream silently.
Down through the centuries
They echo in our hearts and minds
Who love humanity and give price
To the value of freedom.
Their stilled voices send their commands,
"Stay strong in the face of the evil one,
Who schemes and plots the demise of both.
Don't allow the assignments of his dark pride
To overcome your resolve and halt your advance,
For freedom's sake and the sake of love."
We must hasten to heed their admonitions;
Harness their strength that streams from above,
Plow up the ground that has lain fallow,
Plant our feet solidly on rock's foundation
And face the enemy with courage.
Should we be required to join them,
May our voices be heard among their cries
For the sake of love
And the value of freedom
And the reward of the voices of martyrs.

Revelation 12:10-11, *"And I heard a loud voice saying in heaven, Now is come salvation, and strength, and the kingdom of our God, and the power of His Christ: for the accuser of our brethren is cast down, which accused them before our God day and night. [11] And they overcame him by the blood of the Lamb, and by the word of their testimony; and they loved not their lives unto the death."* KJV

Revelation 17:6a, *"And I saw the woman drunken with the blood of the saints, and with the blood of the martyrs of Jesus:..."* KJV

Revelation 22:12, [Jesus said], *"And, behold, I come quickly; and my reward is with me, to give every man according as his work shall be."* KJV

WEEPING IN THE HEAVENS

There is weeping in the heavens,
Do you hear the angels crying?
The turn of mankind away from the Light
Has sparked alarm among helping spirits.
Their tears fall for wayward men
Who abandon their little children.
Their tears fall for the women
Who desire to have no children.
They weep for those who see no need
Nor love to be in the Lord's presence.
They grieve for those who cannot abide
Even one minute past the appointed hour
Church clocks chime for closing prayer.
Cut back on the songs, they demand,
Shorten the sermon, they command,
We mustn't be late for noonday lunch,
The restaurants will be overcrowded.
No, heaven forbid we should occupy
A church pew seat of a worship service
Or listen to God's Word being preached
Beyond the hour the committee has set.
It's more than our endurance can take;
Let us out or we won't return, they say,
After all, ninety minutes is long enough.

No wonder abortions flourish
And men become deadbeat Dads.
No wonder there is no prayer in schools
Nor crosses displayed on mountain tops.
No wonder the crime rate soars
And government sinks deeper in debt.
Too few understand life's principles
Nor can they quote any Scriptures.

It's so much trouble to sit in a church
And try to listen and not complain
That you're missing the football game
Or a trip to the lake with the boat.
Who has time for God anymore?
In the heavens, the angels weep.

Revelation 3:2-3, *"Wake up, and strengthen the things which remain, which were about to die; for I have not found your deeds completed in the sight of My God. ³Remember therefore what you have received and heard; and keep it, and repent. If therefore you will not wake up, I will come like a thief, and you will not know at what hour I will come upon you."* NASB

"What Meaneth This?"

Stay on your toes, red-tie and dark-suited one.
Are you selling or buying?
Are you producing or consuming?
Are you becoming more dependent;
Expecting, anticipating, demanding
Your larder to be made full by others?
"What meaneth this?"
Shouldn't there be a yellow caution sign,
"Warning: The world is falling asleep!"
The signals are flashing before you,
Obvious to the observant eye;
Its pulse and breathing are slowed,
Its muscles weakened, deteriorated.
Its mentality has swept away the rules;
Absolved everything and gained nothing.
Wake up, now! Listen to the herald's call
To reject the dying world
And kick out the ruling beast.
Strengthen your heart once again;
Stand up, rise upon your toes once more.
Stretch your arms heavenward
And call out from anguished man's folly;
"Come, Lord God, and rescue me!"
Let there be shame, then let there be purpose.
What has been lost will be regained;
A day's work, a day's wage,
Your hand, your heart, your desire
To give, to serve, to love.

Proverbs 14:12, *"There is a way which seems right to a man, But its end is the way of death."* NASB
Ephesians 5:13-14, *"But all things become visible when they are exposed by the light, for everything that becomes visible is light. [14]For*

this reason it says, 'Awake, sleeper, And rise from the dead, And Christ will shine on you.'" NASB

Revelation 2:4-5a, "But I have this against you, that you have left your first love. ⁵ᵃRemember therefore from where you have fallen, and repent and do the deeds you did at first;" NASB

Romans 12:1-2, "I beseech you therefore, brethren, by the mercies of God, that you present your bodies a living sacrifice, holy, acceptable unto God, which is your reasonable service. ²And be not conformed to this world: but be transformed by the renewing of your mind, that you may prove what is that good, and acceptable, and perfect will of God." NKJV

Psalm 141:1-2, "O Lord, I call upon Thee; hasten to me! Give ear to my voice when I call to Thee! ²May my prayer be counted as incense before Thee; The lifting up of my hands as the evening offering." NASB

Whispers of Love

Whispers of love float down through the ages.
The big round moon softly speaks the words
Mouthed in the shine of its beams of light
That shimmer and reflect upon the gentle sea.
Under the darkening skies overhead
The words sparkle
As if a flute were playing
With every ripple upon the surface
Where the ocean's gentle breezes waft by.
Then the words burst through ever stronger
When the white foam crashes
And bathes the protruding boulders,
Staggered and stacked at ocean's edge.
The waters recede and reveal wet-soaked sand
Waiting to squish between the toes
Of a lonely stroller.

Comes finally the searching heart
At late night's hour
Sauntering slowly, seeking, longing,
Waiting for the gentle words.
At last, the message of the night
Is left in the footsteps
That trail her closely behind, oh, so briefly,
Until they pool with water
And are swept away
Carrying the message back into the sea.

Love words were here, too quickly gone,
They float back into the heavens above
To be whispered once more
Into the receding night
For another lonesome heart

Who needs to hear the words
Through the twinkling of the stars,
The reflections of the moon,
The visions of the night
Cast upon the sea
Holding, cradling the whispers of the ages,
The whispers of love;
"I love you."

John 3:16, *"For God so loved the world that He gave His only begotten Son, that whosoever believes in Him should not perish, but have everlasting life."* KJV

Who Are You Robin Hood?

Was Robin Hood the original Socialist;
Robbing the rich to give to the poor?
Was he into redistributing the wealth,
Or was he rectifying wrongs
Making himself a true altruist?
What does it mean, *"Thou shalt not steal?"*
Does it mean you should be called a thief
Under any and all circumstances
Whenever you take what is not yours,
Or are there exceptions?
Can thievery's motives be pure and qualified?
Tell me Robin Hood, can stealing be justified?
Or is stealing anything for any reason
In fact *"stealing,"* and begs the question
That makes you a prospect
For hanging on the cross next to Jesus?
Didn't the thief on the cross with repentant heart
Acknowledge his stealing deeds
And recognize his punishment was just and fair?
What of Friar Tuck who tagged along
Giving his blessing to Robin Hood's gang?
Where was his heart;
With the righteous or with the poor?
Or does poor mean righteous
And wealthy mean thief?

Oh, wayward world that defines and redefines
By made-up stories and fantasies;
You seek to right the wrongs and
Make your own wrongs the right.
Who are you, Robin Hood?
Are you the one who denies a thief
The right of repentance nod

To enter the pearly gates of heaven
Where the answer is known to the question;
"What does it mean, '*Thou shalt not steal?*'"

Leviticus 19:11, *"You shall not steal, neither deal falsely, neither lie one to another."* NKJV

Romans 13:9-10, *"For this, 'You shall not commit adultery, you shall not murder, You shall not steal, You shall not covet,' and if there is any other commandment, it is summed up in this saying, 'You shall love your neighbor as yourself.' [10]Love does no wrong to a neighbor; love therefore is the fulfillment of the law."* NASB

WHO CARES?

Who cares about you, sir,
You with the matted hair and beard?
You look like a prehistoric cave-dweller
As you roam the dusty courtyard
Of this men's-only Mexican prison
In diapered underpants and a bared chest.
The question erupts again and again,
Who cares? Does anyone care about you?
A wild look transitions your eyes,
One moment you see me, then you don't.
Who stares back at me or is it what?

Before me rise two-story prison cells
Filled with men wedged together;
There is no room to lie down for sleep.
Men's arms extend wildly through the bars,
Reaching for humanity, reaching for life.
What is left for them is nothing humane;
Only want and need and pain exists.
Hunger growls from deep inside them
And masks their faces with pleading stares.
Nudging, pushing, shoving, the men grunt;
No words are spoken, just snarls and cries
Escape their lips past dark-stained teeth.

Who cares about you incarcerated ones
With unshaven faces and odorous breath?
You sit or stand in filth with torn clothing
Which barely covers your loins and arms.
Only a few of you can sit before the bars
With enough space to thrust out your legs
To dangle your dirt-encrusted, bare feet.
Sunbeams strike your unshaven faces,

Sweat travels down from your brows,
Drips into your squinted, unseeing eyes
And streaks your weather-worn cheeks.
The drenching rivulets of perspiration
Intermingle with tears of silent anguish.
Abandoned to your displays of emotion,
You are indifferent toward visitors,
Those who notice you have lost all pride,
All signs of dignity, civility and freedom
To a meager existence of simply breathing.
Again the question begs, "Who cares?"

Words move past my constricted throat
And at last they begin to escape my lips;
"Listen to me, sir, listen, gentlemen!
In this stench-filled, inhumane place,
This place that seems God-forsaken;
There is a God Who has not forsaken.
You are not forgotten, nor left behind.
The key is not lost nor thrown away;
He has and is your key to freedom,
He will unlock your heart, set you free.
Cry out to the Lord in one sincere prayer,
Then you will soar upon its wings and
Discover it is the Lord Who cares."

2 Peter 3: 9, *"The Lord is not slack concerning His promise, as some men count slackness; but is longsuffering to us-ward, not willing that any should perish, but that all should come to repentance."* KJV
1 Peter 5:6-7, *"Humble yourselves therefore under the mighty hand of God, that He may exalt you in due time:* [7]*Casting all your care upon Him; for He cares for you."* NKJV

My King

It is so easy to kneel before our King,
He is majestic and royal and sovereign;
Since He created us, we belong to Him.
The light that shines before us is His;
It never dims nor fails to be our beacon.
He directs us on a path that's noble,
A moral path, true, dutiful and loyal.
Though it may be a narrow way
And sometimes treacherous;
His protecting hand never lets go.
Feet may stumble, knees be scraped,
A broken bone or torn heart may occur;
But healing flows from His bloody side
To repair, renew and invigorate
For the rest of the journey ahead of us.

He carries a strong shield, unbendable,
A long, sharp sword and His eyes are fire;
All enemies fear our Guardian
Who accompanies our everyday trek.
There is no cause for us to cower;
Be intimidated or ever fearful,
When firey darts are flung toward us.
He spreads a garden before our eyes;
Luscious fruit are ours by choice,
A provision so vast it spreads endlessly
Accompanied by a free-flowing river
That forever quenches a thirsty heart.

Beyond description is my King,
His beauty is perfection and so pure;
Yet He chose this one, less than whole,
To make me His; make me royal

And call me His own; He is my brother,
My loving King Who is full of grace.
His Eternal Name bears mercy; it
Abides within His bejeweled crown.
His Name is lovely, soft and sweet;
His Name is Jesus, my God and King.
His voice is strong with authority,
His face shines like the noonday sun.
Could anyone not hunger for His love?
He always existed, He is and will be;
The beginning and the never-ending,
His kingdom with subjects uncountable;
How easy it is to honor Him, the Christ;
I kneel before my King!

Psalm 95:6, *"Come, let us worship and bow down; Let us kneel before the Lord our Maker."* NASB
Philippians 2:9-11, *"Therefore also God highly exalted Him, and bestowed on Him the name which is above every name,* [10] *that at the name of Jesus every knee should bow, of those who are in heaven, and on earth, and under the earth,* [11] *and that every tongue should confess that Jesus Christ is Lord, to the glory of God the Father."* NASB
Revelation 19:16, *"And on His robe and on His thigh He has a name written, 'KING OF KINGS, AND LORD OF LORDS.'"* NASB

ALL GLORY BE GIVEN TO GOD, THE FATHER,
ALL GLORY IS DUE TO JESUS CHRIST, THE SON,
ALL GLORY AND THANKS BE TO HOLY SPIRIT
FOREVER AND EVER! AMEN!

Psalm 65

1 There will be silence before
Thee, and praise in Zion, O God;
And to Thee the vow will be performed.
2 O Thou who dost hear prayer,
To Thee all men [all flesh] come.
3 Iniquities prevail against me;
As for our transgressions,
Thou dost forgive them.
4 How blessed is the one whom
Thou dost choose, and bring near to Thee,
To dwell in Thy courts.
We will be satisfied with the goodness of
Thy house, Thy holy temple.
5 By awesome deeds Thou dost answer us in
Righteousness, O God of our salvation,
Thou who art the trust of all the ends of the earth
And of the farthest sea;
6 Who dost establish the mountains by His strength,
Being girded with might;
7 Who dost still the roaring of the seas,
The roaring of their waves,
And the tumult of the peoples.
8 And they who dwell in the ends of the earth
Stand in awe of Thy signs;
Thou dost make the dawn and
The sunset shout for joy.
9 Thou dost visit the earth, and cause it to overflow;
Thou dost greatly enrich it;
The stream [the river] of God is full of water;
Thou dost prepare their grain,
For thus Thou dost prepare the earth.
10 Thou dost water its furrow abundantly;
Thou dost settle its ridges;
Thou dost soften it with showers;

Thou dost bless its growth.
11 Thou hast crowned the year with Thy bounty,
And Thy paths drip with fatness.
12 The pastures of the wilderness drip,
And the hills gird themselves with rejoicing.
13 The meadows are clothed with flocks,
And the valleys are covered with grain;
They shout for joy, yes, they sing. NASB

CPSIA information can be obtained at www.ICGtesting.com
Printed in the USA
LVOW12s0306061114

412190LV00001B/1/P